FOOD WAS HER COUNTRY

Dagger Editions is an imprint of Caitlin Press.
8100 Alderwood Road, Halfmoon Bay, BC V0N 1Y1
www.daggereditions.com

Text design by Vici Johnstone. Cover design by Gerilee McBride.
Printed in Canada

Caitlin Press Inc. acknowledges financial support from the Government
of Canada and the Canada Council for the Arts, and the Province of
British Columbia through the British Columbia Arts Council and the
Book Publisher's Tax Credit.

Library and Archives Canada Cataloguing in Publication
Bociurkiw, Marusya, 1958-, author
        Food was her country : the memoir of a queer daughter /
Marusya Bociurkiw.

ISBN 978-1-987915-64-8 (softcover)
        1. Bociurkiw, Marusya, 2. Bociurkiw, Marusya,
1958- —Family. 3. Mothers and daughters—Canada—Biography.
4. Authors, Canadian (English)—Biography. 5. Lesbian authors—
Canada—Biography. 6. Motion picture producers and directors—
Canada—Biography. I. Title.

PS8553.O4Z464 2018   C818'.5409   C2017-
906532-7

FOOD WAS HER COUNTRY
THE MEMOIR OF A QUEER DAUGHTER

MARUSYA BOCIURKIW

Dagger Editions

Praise for *Food Was Her Country*

An un-put-down-able memoir! Daughter Marusya and mother Vera carry food while traversing "spaces large as continents" between them—to find love, grief and love again.

—Cynthia Flood, author of *What Can You Do*

Sharp, tender and affecting, these stories of food and family—and politics and secrets and silence and speech and forgiveness and love—accrue into a powerful whole that left me sad, yearning and satisfied all at once.

—Anne Fleming, author of *poemw*

For all the queer daughters

CONTENTS

ACKNOWLEDGMENTS

This book originated with a food blog, *Recipes for Trouble,* that existed for seven years. Many thanks to all the readers from around the world who lurked, commented, or complained when I didn't post regularly: you were a life force.

Thanks to manuscript readers Penny Goldsmith, Taras Bociurkiw, Carolyn Gammon and Jen Chambers; to Jacob Scheier for helpful commentary; and to the Write or Die women's writing group for feedback and sisterly support over its four years of existence.

This book took its time getting out into the world; thus, I am grateful to those who still saw me as a writer and artist first, even if I didn't: Jennifer Fisher, Cynthia Flood, Lisa Grekul, Halya Kuchmij, the late Haida Paul, and, again and always, Penny Goldsmith. Also, thanks to the Can Serrat International Artists' Residency where this manuscript first took shape, amid the blossoming almond trees and beautiful aromas of Catalan cooking. Thanks as well to those who provided hospitality, food, and space to think, write and play: Jeanette Reinhardt and Glen Sanford of Fanny Bay, BC; Donna Drury and Marie-Andrée Thifault of Montréal, Quebec; Marc Cannon and Mary Daniel of Portland, Ontario. To my family for enduring and sometimes even enjoying my stories about them, and to Michael Bociurkiw for the much-extended loan of my mother's recipe book (thanks bro!). To Anne Shepherd, who provided analysis and maternal affect when it was most needed. To my team at the Studio for Media Activism and

Critical Thought, who help me make sense of the academic/ artist's life; to my students at Ryerson and York universities, who make me hope for the future; and to my friends in Toronto and around the world, who help me to live mindfully in the present.

I am grateful to those who published some of the stories in this book: The CBC Canada Writes Literary Award, and Lisa Grekul and Lindy Ledohowski, editors of the award-winning collection *Unbound: Ukrainian Canadians Writing Home*. Also thanks to the Draft Reading Series, where I got to read a story from this book to the warmest, coziest audience ever.

In this troubling era, it is a privilege to be published by a queer press. Thanks to Vici Johnstone, publisher and visionary founder of Dagger Editions, and to the staff of Caitlin Press. Much gratitude to editor Yvonne Blomer for her patient, thoughtful and transformative commentary. Extra-special thanks to literary consultant Sally Keefe-Cohen, for her staunch belief in this book over many years, and for bringing it home.

Certain names in this book have been changed to protect privacy. The exceptions are public figures, those who have granted permission for their names to be used, the dead and my family. Any inaccuracies, elaborations and exaggerations are entirely my own. It must be said that not all my siblings agree with my version of family events. As much as possible, I have taken this into account. As my mother once said, *That's how it is. Every book's like that.*

Finally, and again, gratitude to my mother, for being there so fully that I had to write about it. *Vichnaya Pamyat.*

1.

FIVE THOUSAND MILES: HERE AND THERE

Here is a square stucco bungalow, suburban street curving like a question mark, trees like misplaced commas, land spread out like a run-on sentence. Edmonton, Alberta: five thousand miles from *there*: the tilting, metal-roofed cottage with white-washed walls, towering poplars and snappish, wandering geese in Schvaikivtsi, Ukraine, where my mother was born.

Here is the feel of the stucco, its itchy imprint on the backs of my bare legs, as friends and I played a girls' game involving a rubber ball placed in the bottom of a nylon stocking. That weighted stocking swung like a weapon between and around arms, legs, and the stucco wall, in approximate rhythm to a rhyming song:

> Miss Mary Mack, Mack, Mack
> All dressed in black, black, black
> With silver buttons, buttons, buttons all down her back, back, back
> She asked her mother, mother, mother, for fifty cents, cents, cents
> To see the elephants, elephants, elephants jump over the fence, fence, fence.

How many times did Mama go to put on nylon stockings and find just one? Did she mutter curse words and, for the millionth time, lament that the Pope did not permit birth control? I consider what the smashing ball and the relentless narrative of *Miss Mary Mack Mack Mack* must have sounded like from inside the house while Mama cooked pork chops and scalloped potatoes for dinner, mixed with the sound of sizzling onions, my brothers' fighting and the national news on a TV always left on, like an eternal flame.

Here is a typical dinner conversation, sometime in the 1970s: rudimentary, with great dollops of insult and sarcasm.

Me: *Pass the salt.*

Roman: *Why should I?*

Me: *Because I asked you.* (In Ukrainian) *DAD, Roman won't pass me the salt!*

My father: (In Ukrainian) *Silence! I had more peace in the concentration camp!*

Michael: *Are there any more cabbage rolls?*

Jeannie: *Gimme the roast beef.*

Me: (In Ukrainian) *Tato, can you drive me to Halya's house?*

My father: (In Ukrainian) *When?*

Jeannie: *As if!* (In Ukrainian) *She's not going to Halya's house. She's going out to a movie with her English friends!*

Me: *Shut up.*

Me: (In Ukrainian) *Dad, how about now? You can just drop me off at the mall.*

My father: (In Ukrainian) *OK.*

My mother: (In Ukrainian) *Absolutely NOT.*

Jeannie: *Ha ha!*

Whatever might be said about the level of discourse at our kitchen table, there was always dinner, and our parents were always there.

My oldest brother Taras, known then as Terry, was, to me, unknowable. Seven years older than me, he wasn't usually at the table. As a child, I knew him as a tough babysitter and a cool easy rider — he motorcycled across Europe when he was twenty. In the home movies, he is constantly smirking, clowning for the camera, always ridiculous.

Jeannie was my nemesis. We shared a bedroom into her teens and my preteens. I still have nightmares about the mine-field of our shared closet, me borrowing her mod clothes (if borrowing means taking without asking), her ratting on me. Jeannie was goody-two-shoes, making me, the only other daughter at the time, the bad girl. I resented it, not yet under-standing that that label would be my ticket to freedom.

If I was the bad daughter, Roman was the bad son, desig-nated troublemaker and family iconoclast. The family photos show him scowling, crying, trying always to run off, bent to-ward liberty in every way. What Roman really was, was highly sensitive, with an artist's instinct for authenticity. He became a talented musician, famous in his way. If only we'd known then what we know now.

Michael was the baby of the family at the time (Lydia, currently the youngest, hadn't been born yet). Sweet and a little bit show-offy, he was coddled by my mother and occa-sionally mocked by my father. I think that incomprehensible (for a child) dichotomy stays with him even now. I adored him, but I was aware that he lived in a rarefied world of in-dulgence.

Parenting wasn't a thing then, Dr. Spock notwithstanding. My parents didn't read books about how to raise children, trou-bled or otherwise, and they certainly didn't discuss such matters with others. Children in a large middle-class family like ours were kind of servant class. You couldn't bring up six kids any other way. Think of it: no daycare (although my mother did eventually create a Ukrainian playschool), no counselling, no special needs teachers, unless you had an extreme disability.

We were loved, in a hard-bitten, inflexible, possessive way. Love that was shaped by peasant villages, by long-ago hungers, by forced migration, by boats and trains, by how you had to be constantly vigilant so your kids wouldn't fall from the narrow path you'd been afforded. Funny how that kind of love trickles through your bloodstream and informs your adult life. It made me into a tough-lover of kids, a teacher and a mentor with high expectations, love humming inaudibly in the background.

There was always dinner, six nights a week, fifty-two weeks of the year. There were pork chops; there were Porcupine Meatballs in Tomato Sauce, Meat Loaf Deluxe, and Chinese Salad, whose mismatched ingredients included iceberg lettuce and canned water chestnuts. There were perogies and cabbage rolls to be sure, but there was also Whip 'n Chill Chocolate Pudding on weekdays, and my own controversial, elaborate confections on Sundays. For lunch, often prepared by my working-at-home professor dad: pleasantly slimy Chef Boyardee spaghetti from a can; on weekends, Chef Boyardee pizza, upon whose readymade crust we gleefully assembled canned pepperoni and sauce. All through the short, hot Alberta summer, there was Taber corn, glistening with margarine, stuccoed with salt, illuminating our faces with grease.

My mother landed in Canada as a young child. The five thousand miles were of little or no import to her, as evinced by the wide-ranging ethnic affiliations of her recipe book (Sole Bonne Femme and Colcannen make appearances), her perfect, unaccented English and the way she spoke French, like it was her mother tongue.

Mama learned French as a girl in a convent school in Morinville, Alberta. She liked to remind us, rather frequently, smugly, even: *That convent was like heaven to me.* She adored anything French, and she loved Canada, with its shopping malls and well-stocked Safeway stores. For my father the post-war refugee, the miles were an ache, a heartbreak, a brutal life lesson that could never really be mastered, even with a Ph.D. Over Mama's intricately assembled German Rouladen (beef wrapped around bacon, onions and mustard), he told us gruesome, unbelievable stories about a long-ago concentration camp, the potato-peel soup they ate there, and his escape, carried through the Bavarian forest on the shoulders of an older man. My father had been twenty at the time.

As a child I ate whatever was placed in front of me but did whatever I pleased with my imagination. While gulping back Chicken Paprikash with egg noodles, iceberg salad on the side, I compared it to Tato's potato-peel soup and felt a kind of cheeriness at my father's heroic survival and thus, my existence. I was maybe the only kid on the block who lay awake at night rehearsing what she'd say to Nazis and/or Bolsheviks, when they came banging on our door. Would I capitulate immediately, turning in my little brothers Roman and Mikey, or would I be a martyr, refusing to name names, like the dissidents Grigorenko, Chornovil and Solzhenitsyn?

Despite my mother's best culinary efforts, my father's trauma flavoured our food with the sour tang of remorse. Bitter aromas flared like burnt toast, making my parents argue, making me feel like a traitor for leaving the house to watch TV with my Anglo friends. Guilt followed me everywhere I went: on the bus to school, or down the stairs to my friends' rumpus rooms. Guilt for leaving, even for an evening; for having fun; for not wanting to come home.

Five thousand miles. What was the point of them?

There were letters from the old country, with spidery writing on blue parchment, sometimes accompanied by packages of dried mushrooms blooming with a dusky stink. There was a national poet (Taras Shevchenko), whose greatest hits we memorized in Ukrainian, exhorting us to rise up, break our chains and sprinkle our freedom with the enemy's blood. There was summer camp, a fusion of scouting tradition and rebel army, where we were roused in the middle of the night to do war games. There was the brick Byzantine church we went to every Sunday, a long-haired Old Testament God glaring at us from inside the dome, perpetually angry, with a long yellow hipster beard and hands raised like a boogeyman, shocking us into piety. (According to church lore, the original painting was even scarier, and had to be toned down so as not to "inspire dread.")

Nothing was normal, and nothing ever would be.

There was an Iron Curtain (which I believed to be an actual, very unwieldy curtain), and Soviet stamps, and Russia, to which we were supposed to hate. We were born in Canada, which was solid and bright, but there was this other place, *the Ukraine*, five thousand miles away, where old babas lined up for bread, and it was sad, and we were supposed to love it. On feast days, we sang Ukraine's national anthem, "*Sche Ne Vmerla Ukraina*" (Ukraine Has Not Yet Died), which made me shiver with embarrassment. On Saturdays, after a pilgrimage to the Polish delicatessen, we memorized complex verb declensions at Ukrainian school and on Sundays we had church, the graveyard, *Walt Disney, Bonanza*. When kids at school asked me what I did on the weekend, I made sure to change the subject.

Whether through food or writing or dreams, I have been traversing those five thousand miles, not quite here and never really there, ever since. The journey is illusory, a play with hyphens and hybridity, with desire and disavowal; Rushdie's imaginary homelands: part fiction, part documentary, all story.

My mother has travelled with me, almost all the way.

A GIRL, WAITING

As a teenager, I went through a dessert-making phase as festive as it was grim.

My father had taken a job at Carleton University, and so we moved to Ottawa from Edmonton the day Neil Armstrong landed on the moon. The house was newly built, the land around it naked as a lunar landscape. We watched Armstrong hop around in his space suit, while Michael earnestly took photos of the TV screen.

Through an upstairs window, I spent hours watching our neighbours cavort in their backyard swimming pool: exotic English banter, blonde hair, good-natured mom and dad. The rest of my time was spent in the kitchen, baking.

The 1970s were a thrilling era of chiffon pies, extravagant parfaits, and endless variations on Baked Alaska. Not one to miss out on culinary history, I took it upon myself to make dessert for about a year's worth of Sunday lunches for my family.

My preparations began on Saturday, when I accompanied my mother on her weekend shopping trip to Safeway. I was a silent and slouching figure habitually dressed in beatnik black, in the backseat of our red Volvo station wagon. This mute arrangement suited us both, each too dispirited to entertain the remote possibility of civil conversation. As a teenager, I thought silence and depression were status quo and that hours and days of muteness between a mother and her daughter was normal. I thought family was a desert you had to traverse to get to a place where people were curious, and got to know you, and where there was a *you* someone would want to know.

At the glittering supermarket, we immediately parted ways. Off I went to the baking aisle to ogle McCormick Cream of Tartar, Lyle's Golden Syrup and Nabisco Graham Crackers. I lingered over the triumphant inventions of the western world, most of them absent from my mother's pantry. After making my selections, I located my mother dolefully examining brands of liverwurst and pickled herring in the deli section. I dumped my items into her shopping cart, took the keys out of her purse, and didn't look back when she said, loudly and embarrassingly, in Ukrainian, *What is wrong with you?* I returned to the car. The names of those items were the blank verse of a culture — American? English? Normal? — I desperately wanted to speak.

To Mama's credit, I do not recall any of my ingredients, arcane as they were, getting tossed at the cash. Perhaps my mother was bemused by my eccentricity. Perhaps, of all the teenage peccadilloes I might have acquired (drugs, alcohol, an English boyfriend), this one was unbelievably benign.

I chose desserts only from decidedly non-ethnic sources, like *Betty Crocker* or *The Pillsbury Cookbook*. I adored the names of their creations: Tunnel of Fudge Gateau; Strawberry Chiffon Chocolate Pie. I basked in their confidence and scientific prowess: *Every Recipe Perfected For You in Our Test Kitchens* boasted, *Better Homes and Gardens New Cook Book*. "It is our sincere wish that this cookbook may be of assistance to the women of Canada," proclaimed *The Blue Ribbon Cookbook*. Indeed, the good people at *Blue Ribbon* had taken it upon themselves to instruct Canadian housewives on menu-planning. Every meal was to have one hot dish. Variety was crucial ("A meal where everything is whitish is unappetizing.") Highly spiced foods and pickles were to be sparingly served. *The Modern Encyclopedia of Cooking* even instructed housewives on The Social Use of Food: "The dinner table is no place for any member of the family to air the grievances of the day, for the husband to take his wife to task for extravagance, for the wife to express her financial worries, for either of them to scold or discipline the children."

My father was often belligerent at the table, and we kids felt no compunction in airing the grievances of the day. I was mortified by the plate of my Mama's homemade dill pickles at every meal, the cold breakfasts, the whitish meals of perogies and sour cream. Dessert would be my corrective. Thus, on Saturday nights, while my female peers were going to movies, having sleepovers, or engaging in the sweet, awkward rituals of dating, or the sweaty exigencies of teenage sex, I, like some miniature gay man, made dessert.

My baking binges took hours, sometimes days. I was enamoured of complex, multi-valenced concoctions, preferably those, like my beloved Baked Alaska, which involved both baking and freezing. Extremes of temperature and flavour were my specialty.

I had not yet resolved the uncertainties of my libido, was secretly worried about my profound disinterest in the junior high prom. It would be a quarter century before *Will and Grace* and *Ellen* appeared on my television screen. Were the assertive flavours and temperatures of Fudge Ribbon Pie metaphor for my unacknowledged desires?

The making of Fudge Ribbon Pie begins relatively casually, with the combining of unsweetened chocolate squares and evaporated milk. Butter, sugar and vanilla are stirred in, after which the mixture is cooled.

And then, all hell breaks loose. "Spoon half of the peppermint ice cream into a cooled pastry shell," orders the cookbook, shrilly. "Cover with half the cooled chocolate sauce; freeze. Repeat with the remaining ice cream and sauce. Cover and freeze overnight."

As if these hours of blending, rolling, baking, stirring, spooning, freezing, spooning and freezing again were not sufficient workout for a lanky, depressive teenage girl with hormones to burn, there was still the meringue: three egg whites beaten with vanilla and cream of tartar. "Gradually add 6 tablespoons sugar, beating till stiff and glossy peaks form," demanded the cookbook in its relentless fashion. And then: "Fold 3 tablespoons of crushed peppermint-stick candy into the meringue."

By then, my family had returned from church (I stayed in bed as they left, feigning a coma). My father, due to my utter lack of religiosity, was now shunning me. Mama heated roast beef, gravy and mashed potatoes in static, bristling silence, no doubt disturbed by my territorial incursion and its perceived critique of her cuisine. Roman, Mikey, Jeannie and Lydia were exhausted from a half-hour each way of fighting in the car, followed by ninety minutes of Byzantine Ukrainian Catholic worship, with its chronic standing and kneeling, its kissing of crosses and beating of chests. They were irritated and unsettled by a rambling sermon chastising them for every biological and psychological desire imaginable, delivered by a beet-faced priest desperate for his noontime glass of wine.

In short, my audience, as I removed the pie from the freezer, spread the meringue over the chocolate layer, sprinkled the top with a remaining 1 tablespoon of crushed candy, placed the pie, for reasons unknown, on an old, unfinished wooden cutting board, and baked at 475 degrees for 4 to 5 minutes or until golden, serving at once, was less than ideal. By now they were soporific from their whitish servings of perogies, roast beef on the side, pickles on the side of that. My father, a diabetic, and my mother, a devotee of Weight Watchers, eyed my pie with fascinated revulsion.

My siblings consumed their enormous slices of Fudge Ribbon Pie in silence, and then left the table without a word. What could they do? The pie's pop culture American flavours were delectable to them, but my mother's disapproval transformed it into contraband. Mama had long since disappeared from the kitchen. Only my father and I were left at the table. He, freed from his wife's watchful gaze, was digging into a second slice, smiling guiltily at me. I, coming down from the high of baking and serving, was left with an addict's aftertaste: pride mixed with shame; cold and hot, juxtaposed.

After my year of extreme desserts ended, I entered into a decade-long dalliance with heterosexuality. I went on a handful of dates with theatrical boys; boys who read Nietszche; boys who sang in the church choir. One hundred percent of them turned out to be gay.

Who lives in silence and who gets to speak? I no longer disavow the girl who stood so silently and unhappily over the simmering pot of chocolate, waiting for the right texture to appear. I suspect the hot and cold temperatures, the desperate sweetness of those long-ago Sunday confections to be a language more genuine than speech.

Perhaps only my mother understood who I really was: a girl waiting and waiting, with regret and excitement — for subways and rented rooms, for cities and cabarets — for her life to begin.

FOOD WAS HER COUNTRY

The Vegetarian Epicure was my very first cookbook. My copy, published in 1972, cost me $5.95, brand new. In her introduction, the author, Anna Thomas, promised that a vegetarian epicure would find the satisfaction of feeling a peaceful unity with all life. Not bad, for just six bucks.

Peaceful unity was thin on the ground in Alta Vista, an Ottawa suburb where no vista existed. My high school marks were abysmal, and teachers' comments were not flattering: "Though not without some ability," wrote one such teacher, "Marusya is somewhat lethargic towards her education."

Indeed, I moved very slowly through the world. I had *ennui*. Doing my hair and makeup took everything I had. I no longer cooked dessert or, indeed, any sort of dish for my family. I had bigger fish to fry. I was reading Virginia Woolf and Anaïs Nin, my literary soulmates. My family fell far short of Woolf's cool crowd in Bloomsbury, or Nin's sexual sophistication, her "bi-coastal trapeze." I understood there to be a bohemian movement, somewhere downtown, and I felt its tidal, oceanic pull.

And that was how I ended up at a macrobiotic dinner, at the beginning of my seventeenth year. It had been advertised at the health food store (where I purchased my contraband granola and yogurt) on a faded xeroxed piece of paper pinned to a bulletin board:

Macrobiotic Discussion & Potluck
October 27, 6 p.m.
What has a beginning has an end

I had to lie to my parents and say I was going to some Ukrainian girl's house (which was my free pass to stay out all night if I wanted, and they never checked). I dressed in my best corduroy bell-bottoms, gauzy Indian top and Jesus sandals, braiding my hair like I thought a macrobiotic might, in a corona around my head. The event was in a rural location, not far from Ottawa: I took two buses to get to the highway and then hitchhiked, arriving at dusk at a farmhouse full of strangers. My childhood had given me nothing with which to measure safety, and therefore allowed me great latitude. *When I was your age, I had already been through a war,* my father used to say. Hitching alone at twilight was the least I could do to measure up. It was thrilling, narrowly escaping a highway kidnapping (or worse), then walking into a living room with no furniture, just batik pillows and a thick fog of pot smoke, people in dirty jeans and political-message T-shirts, sitting cross-legged on the floor.

Macrobiotics, though I didn't know it then, was cutting-edge. Brought to North America from Japan by Michio and Aveline Kushi, it was the first contemporary Western locavore and vegan food movement. It combined the spiritual (a hybrid of Buddhism, Taoism and others) with the practical. The balancing of yin and yang (acid and alkaline) in the food we ate that night was meant to elevate consciousness and heal the body of everything from tension to cancer.

All I knew was that Yoko Ono and John Lennon were macriobiotic, and that was enough for me. In that antediluvian era before Instagram and Facebook, the health food stores of downtown Ottawa were my portal into the racy world of anti-war, lefty and sexual politics. Their bulletin boards introduced me to the unheard-of, indeed, the highly forbidden: *Vegetarian Co-op House! Anti-War-Teach-In! Radical Lesbian Potluck!*

The food at that long-ago dinner featured miso soup, boiled chick peas, brown rice, tahini sauce, wild mushroom stew and even seaweed pie. The repast was entirely beige and smelled a little like soiled underwear. For someone brought up on the dill-and-paprika-seasoned meat and potato dishes of Eastern Europe, it was also impressively flavourless. It felt like I could escape the Ukrainian diaspora really soon.

I sat down carefully on the floor with my plate full of food. I smiled brightly. No one spoke or even smiled at me. (Did I have suburb written all over me?). Did people notice that I, who thought potluck meant something like "gathering," or "hootenanny," had come empty-handed? Or maybe it was because, according to macrobiotic protocol, you had to chew each mouthful at least fifty times, leaving absolutely no room for small talk. A culinary heathen, I had stumbled into the Orthodox Religion of vegetarianism. My stomach ached from the tension of it all.

I felt a sudden, unaccustomed longing for my mother's kitchen, stinking of garlic, onions and meat, where we would all argue about Soviet Communism with raised and sometimes angry voices. It was where I'd grown accustomed to defending Women's Liberation (it was International Women's Year; I had the official poster in my room) to my father and brothers, mouth full of pork hocks and sauerkraut. The flavours of my mother's food would linger on my tongue long after dinner was over. When Mama cooked, I never felt hungry afterwards.

Still ravenous, I left the macrobiotic dinner before dessert (carob brownies), got a ride back into town with a moody civil servant and was home by nine, in time to make myself a Havarti-on-rye sandwich, pickles on the side, and watch *The Avengers* with my dad.

My mom came downstairs just as *The Avengers* was ending. She was wearing her floral housecoat and there were curlers in her hair. She looked at me and then looked away. Food was her country.

She had x-ray eyes. She could see everything.

My mother took my empty plate and put it in the kitchen sink.

ONE DARK SUBURBAN NIGHT

The Vegetarian Epicure was about as far from macrobiotics as you could get. Its recipes were over-the-top lavish and creamy. The author was of Polish descent, so dishes like Russian Vegetable Pie, Blini and, bizarrely, Potato Peel Broth, provided some measure of continuity with my childhood. Unlike so many cookbooks, my copy does not contain margin notes or scribbled directives to self. It was my first cookbook, after all, a text too sacred to write in. But the book, battered survivor of eighteen moves, now barely held together with tape, carries its own archive of marks and stains. A corner of the book looks like it got too close to a burner, souvenir of the many dangerously tiny kitchens I cooked in. It seems I was obsessed with pie: Torta di Ricotta, Pastry Brisée, and Zucchini Quiche confess to the most drip marks. The page for Basic Shortcrust Pastry is practically illegible beneath its expressionist composition of dribbles.

The two-page perogy recipe is pristine. With my mother still alive, I had a seemingly endless supply of frozen perogies on hand.

The first item I cooked from *The Vegetarian Epicure* was Stuffed Baked Eggplant.

I'd met a wan, reserved girl named Deidre, hospitalized for anorexia, at the Children's Hospital, where I'd been volunteering. She was about the same age as me. She was tall and had long, stringy blonde hair parted in the middle, framing her angular, serious face. I found her pretty, even though (or perhaps because) she wore the same long-sleeved floral-print granny dress every day. Once, through a half-shut curtain, I caught a glimpse of her shoulder blades, distinct as a pair of boomerangs. Clothed, Deidre looked like Mary Ingalls from *Little House on the Prairie*; close-up, she smelled sweet and sour, like milk gone slightly off. As I did my rounds, I caught her rolling her eyes at the children's magazines I had on offer. One day, I sneaked in a copy of *Cosmopolitan* magazine for her and we talked a bit. It turned out we were both into Anaïs Nin and Women's Lib.

I was fascinated, excited, even. I had never heard of anorexia before. I would gaze covertly at her waxy skin and glassy eyes, which reminded me of my father's wartime stories. Eating disorders made no sense to me: in my family we all stuffed ourselves full of bread, meat and canned vegetables until our stomachs ached.

The day that Deidre was set to be released, I approached her, gingerly. She was sitting on her bed, staring out the window and chewing pensively on a strand of hair. I stood in the doorway.

Hi Deirdre.

Unh, hi. She didn't look at me.

You getting out today?

Yup.

Far out.

Yeah.

Um, can I have your phone number?

Deidre slow-motion shrugged her narrow pointy shoulders, and, like a celebrity, quickly scribbled her phone number on the notebook I proffered with outstretched arm. She never looked at me.

One discreet month later, I called Deidre. Her mother answered.

Hello?

Hi…Can I please speak to Deidre?

Who shall I say is calling please?

Umm, it's her friend. Her friend from the hospital.

The hos-pi-tal?

MOM! It was Deidre, on the extension. *Mom! Hang up please!*

Hi. Hi Deidre! It's. It's Marusya!

Hi Marusya. Her voice was pleasingly dull and uninflected over the phone.

So I dunno I was wondering if you would like to come over for dinner next week to my house I live in Alta Vista I don't know where you live but maybe someone could drive you.

Oh.

Like, really casual.

Oh. Ok.

We agreed on a date and time. I gave her my address. My parents and five siblings were not invited. I have no idea where they all went.

I spent the day cooking. The stuffed eggplants, but also salad and dessert. Deidre arrived right on time. I barely recognized her. The hippie chick I'd grown so fond of had disappeared. The granny outfit had been replaced by a short denim dress with small white buttons all down the front. Her hair had been trimmed into a shag cut with flipped-up bangs, evidence of a curling iron. She wore blue eyeshadow and lip gloss.

I could see the tail lights of her mother's car, blinking anxiously and then disappearing into the dark suburban night.

I ushered Deidre into the dining room. Her eyes widened when she saw a dinner table set only for two.

I served those eggplants quite formally, on my mother's Royal Doulton china, under the dangling dining room chandelier. They were as fat as Dierde was thin; it was as though I wanted to stuff *her*. I poured Black Tower wine into my mother's crystal wineglasses and observed Deidre carefully as we ate.

I can still call forth the pained expression on her face as she diligently swallowed three mouthfuls of stuffed eggplant before calling it quits. She didn't touch the salad or the bread. She asked if she could call her mom. She was out the door before I could serve dessert: apple cake with whipped cream.

Deidre was, I believe, my very first dinner guest. I've had too many awkward dates to count since then. In truth, my mother may have set the pattern. I've always had a thing for women of few words, for reserve, for the champion fight for love.

DEATH WISH

I was eighteen years old. In a car. There were windshield wipers, pointing accusingly. Rain making everything look like a movie flashback. Monochrome, and blurred at the edges. It must have been evening, because *As It Happens* was playing on the car radio, I remember the theme music in counterpart to the swish and swoop of the windshield wipers.

We were talking about health food. Or rather, I was, and my father was half-listening.

You should try brown rice. It's way better for you than white rice.

I make kasha for you in the morning. Isn't that enough?

But I'm talking about you. You eat too much butter and cheese and then all those pills. You could get a heart attack!

Nexai sche die bozha volia. (Let God's will be done.)

What? What are you saying? That you want a heart attack?

Crackling voices debating Canadian foreign policy on the radio. Swish, swoop, rain, rain. A pause.

It is true that I have a death wish.

My father was fifty-one years old. His voice was soft and wistful as he told me this. Like it was the same as wishing for a beautiful painting, or a really superb glass of wine.

It was 1975, some thirty years since my father's own wartime experiences. There had been no therapy, no support groups for this ambitious academic and father of six. I now know that the phrase "death wish" derives from Freud, who worked with survivors of World War 1. In his essay "Mourning and Melancholia," Freud argued that when mourning was unresolved it became melancholia (now known as a form of depression): a loss of self-worth, and an overcoming of "the instinct which compels every living thing to cling to life."

Unable to resolve his own wartime experience, my father was unable to see worth in even his most extraordinary achievements. Chronically depressed people are hard on themselves, harder on others. Curiously, they also seek to be seen and admired. It is a kind of narcissism.

But as a young girl, I only saw my father as an extension of myself, and as someone who should take care of me. I knew he had a bad heart. Was overweight. Ate a lot of really high fat food, took pills for blood pressure and for sleep. His death wish was completely attainable, as far as I could see.

In conversation with my brother Taras, many years later, we discuss whether such a statement could have been metaphor; perhaps he was being ironic, or maybe he was just super-depressed that day. *I never heard him say it*, says Taras protectively. But I heard him say it. I was only eighteen. Everything was literal. I could only conclude that death was more appealing to him than driving me places, arguing about politics over the dinner table, and helping me with my university application. That it was preferable, even, to our Saturday morning trips to the deli, or our clandestine watching of *The Avengers*, after Mom had gone to bed.

I heard him say all of that.

What could I do but plan for my own survival?

I was awkward. Full of poetry. TV and nature filled me, temporarily. My mother haunted me, day and night: her voice, her silence. What she cooked: hamburgers, pork chops, perogies, borscht. What I ate: a wiener; Melba toast with canned corn on the side.

If I ate like them, I thought like them. If I never got away. Home was house arrest. Home was all the spoken and unspoken messages of trauma. All through those TV-lit suburban nights, I dreamed of escape.

Nathalie Goldberg writes about a suburban childhood as generative: "I had to digest the blandness and desolation of my childhood and make them mine….The suburbs were ideal for developing a life of cloistered aloneness, a monk's or a writer's life…" Amid the cookie-cutter houses, the buzz of lawn mowers and the monotonous petunia beds, I painted apocalyptic landscapes and wrote stories about rebellious girls. An eccentric boy from high school invited me to his house one night and showed me flyers of an art school out east: an internationally recognized centre for conceptual art. I had no idea what conceptualism was, but the school was near the ocean, had a loft you could stay at in New York, and unlike all other art colleges in Canada at the time, granted degrees rather than diplomas (I was a professor's daughter, after all). I applied.

One year after my father told me about his death wish, I packed my bags — just one bag, really—and left. I took a train east, to that art college in Halifax, Nova Scotia. I would leave my father before he left me. I would carry my own baggage, cook my own food, make my own art. My father was, in fact, financing my education. Nonetheless, I was convinced I had to be my own solace, my own companion.

I expanded my culinary skills in that salty maritime town, writing a food story of my very own. The single health food store offered bland, well-meaning bricks of bread, and the bakeries yielded soft, innocuous loaves in shades of white or beige. Aaron Bobrow-Strain, in his social history of bread, writes that, in the 1970s, whole-grain bread became a symbol of the peace, feminist and civil rights movements. *Recipes for a Small Planet* (*High Protein Meatless Cooking!*) provided me with an environmental mandate for vegetarianism and instructed me in the making of long, skinny loaves of whole wheat poppy-seed bread baked in coffee cans.

I was a wide-eyed hippie-ish girl who had never kneaded bread dough in her life. I dashed to school every day in the fog, a huge sketchbook under my arm, stone buildings and gravestones escorting me there. I rented a room in a two-hundred-year-old house on Bishop Street, shared with architecture students, a couple of performance artists and an unemployed vegetarian girl. We took turns cooking meatless meals. One day, it would be quiche (that would be me), the next, a greyish soybean stew (unemployed girl). My room had a working fireplace. You could smell the harbour, just down the road. I could not believe I had escaped the suburbs so easily. Waking up in the morning, on a small, narrow mattress on the floor, a wooden Murchie's tea box as my side table, Ukrainian *kylym* as my blanket, I was giddily grateful for my freedom — my recipe for happiness for a very long time.

At the house next door, the windows sparkled with intertwined women's symbols formed from branches draped in Christmas lights. Dropping by for the first time to borrow sugar, I said to the heavy-set, crewcut woman who answered the door, *I love your window decoration! What does it mean?* My bull-dyke neighbor stared at me with a kind of compassionate horror, backed away to the kitchen, returned with my sugar and firmly shut the door. It would be years before I enjoyed the promise of those women's symbols. I took on macrobiotics instead. My seaweed pie, with its troubling ropy texture, was an aggressive offering, my way of expressing difference without the perogies and the sour cream.

A full two years after I'd moved to Halifax, my father showed up in town. He was attending a big conference of the Learneds Society, now known as the Congress of the Humanities and Social Sciences — a mega-conference for all academics in Canada. That year, it was being hosted at Dalhousie University. It so happened that I had a piece at my college's Anna Leonowens Gallery that same week.

It was the late 1970s, and the art world was in turmoil. I'd long since sold the wooden box of oil paints my father had given me. Conceptual art — work in which the idea is more important than a finished art product — was in vogue. It was a way to intervene into a situation where art had become a commodity, and painters like Jackson Pollock and Barnett Newman were wealthy celebrities. It just wasn't done to paint landscapes anymore.

I was a second-year art student, barely out of my immigrant family teens. I'd been dazzled by two years of art history, by film theory, by Freud, Adorno and Mulvey, by the brash stirrings of feminist art. This was my first exhibited work, titled, simply, "Celluloid." It was comprised of several shots of people crossing the street in Manhattan, using different coloured filters. I'd made the film into a single loop. On the wall, an impenetrable quote from a Marxist film critic about colour as semiotic sign.

My father walked over to the quote first, stared at it, arms behind his back, and then pivoted neatly. He gave his full attention to the film screen, with its relentless march of pedestrians in red, blue, yellow and green. He glanced at me with a raised eyebrow, looked back at the screen and then sat down on the chair I'd provided him. He took off his hat (he always wore a hat). He sighed, deeply and sorrowfully.

You once painted so beautifully, he said.

I remember how angry I was at him, how I berated him over the dinner he treated me to that evening. How he apologized. After years of his distracted parenting, I finally had my father's attention and I could not bear it.

My father's death wish had become my inheritance, something that lived inside me, a kind of pulse. By his comment in that car years earlier, my father had seemed to abandon me. Without even knowing it, I turned his death wish into a gift, or revenge, or maybe a bit of both.

2.

MY MOTHER, MY MUSE

I want to come to your graduation, she announced when I picked up the phone. Skipping the formalities as usual.

Oh, Mom, that's OK. I mean, it's a small graduation and it's in January, it'll probably be raining, actually probably hail, maybe snow, it's been a bad winter…

I'm coming.

But Ma! I wasn't even planning to go!

None of the cool kids went to graduation, and if they did it was to protest art world elitism, or sexism, or capitalism, or all of the above. In any case, what would I tell her about my art piece?

There was silence on the other end of the line. I realized my mother was crying, a rising liquid wave of helpless sobs getting louder and louder. I had never heard this sound from my mother before.

Had something terrible happened? I assumed she was lonely. My father had been travelling a lot. She'd started doing volunteer work with Vietnamese refugees who were arriving in Ottawa in great numbers. Maybe she was burnt out from that. And why wasn't my tato coming too? There was no way to ask. Personal, intimate speech was a language we'd never spoken.

I mentally planned a summit meeting with my roommates. Our filthy three-storey house would need to be sterilized from top to bottom.

Yeah. Sure. OK. Why don't you come?

I had joined the college's Women's Affairs Committee the day I arrived at Nova Scotia College of Art and Design. It was as though a spaceship had picked me up at the Ukrainian church basement and dropped me off on another planet. A planet populated with art students, and even feminists. I could not believe my luck: that I did not have to create a feminist world on my own; that there were women who spoke the same underground dialect as me.

At the first meeting I attended, the committee was planning the year's activities. They seemed like remote goddesses, female students and faculty seated majestically around a conference table, stony expressions on their faces.

Can we have a potluck? I asked eagerly, now that I knew what a potluck was.

Oh. My. God, blurted a willowy, ginger-haired grad student named Susan. She seemed to be the ringleader. She gazed up at the ceiling as though contemplating a long, horrific procession of hummus, soybean casseroles and carob brownies: *Not another potluck,* she groaned.

I sank down into my chair. Apparently, there were far more serious issues to deal with. Our standard art history textbook was the 750-page Janson's *History of Art.* It named not a single woman. Coincidentally or not, almost all of the college's instructors were white men. I watched, fascinated, as the women devised a game plan to win this particular gender war: a yearly film series called *Lifesize: Women and Film,* a long-term strategy to bring in visiting women artists, and a plan to initiate a feminist art course that would, in just a few years, be part of core curriculum. Their sense of entitlement, even their rudeness, was thrilling.

The Women's Affairs Committee was badass. Legend had it that committee members had once snuck into the projection room before an art history class, replacing the usual images with slides of outrageous, explicit art by feminist artists. One day, a year into my studies, Harmony Hammond, a feminist artist from New York, spoke at the college. She brought hundreds more slides of work by feminist artists with her. By then I was a stalwart member of the committee. Susan and I sat side by side in a lecture hall as works by dozens of American feminist artists slid before our eyes, the click of the slide projector and Harmony's gentle voice punctuating our awed silence. There were breasts sculpted onto the walls of a kitchen, brightly coloured brooms cast in plaster as though they were important sculptures, and a grainy performance art photo of a woman scrubbing the floor of an art gallery. Those images changed everything. They gave me permission.

My graduating piece was a series of formal studio portraits of the women in my graduating class, accompanied by rather depressing statistics on women in the art world, and a poster I'd plastered all over campus: a mock job ad, with a cheery photo of me and my roommate Dave.

The Art World.
It May Have a Place for You.

It is not a place for everyone. It is a career for a very few special men and even fewer women with skills and a minimum of talent. Qualifications include: male gender and/or complete identification with masculine aesthetics.

That poster was the first thing my mother saw when she entered the college doors, the day of my convocation. She was wearing a silk dress and a mink coat. My friends who worked in the library beside the front door stared.

What's that. Is that you? she asked.

Yeah. Well, me and Dave. You met him at breakfast.

Dave. He's your boyfriend.

No. No. He's posing. It's like, a fake employment poster.

Hmph. Interesting.

And so, Mama sat with me in the audience at my neo-Marxist art school convocation with a Marxist feminist, artist Martha Rosler, as the guest speaker. My mother listened closely to Martha's address and cried again when Martha sarcastically congratulated all the women in my graduating class, spouting those very same art world statistics.

There was a reception afterwards, in a drawing studio. Artworks from the graduating class on the walls. Oysters and champagne laid out on a long wooden table. I introduced my mother to curious fellow students. She strolled around the room and carefully examined every art piece in the show, as though there would be an exam after.

I stood around awkwardly, covertly glancing at Martha Rosler, wishing I had the guts to talk to her. This was not a problem for Vera. She strode up to Martha, an acclaimed media artist, and asked her to take a mother-daughter photo. This was in the days when few people owned cameras. Martha had one slung over her shoulder. She complied good-naturedly but never sent the picture. Here's what I imagine it looked like: my mother in her best flowered dress, matching earrings and necklace, purse coordinated to her high heels, glaring proudly and defiantly at the camera. Her daughter in an Indian-print tent dress, long frizzy hair and big glasses, an embarrassed smirk on her face.

After graduation, I moved to Toronto. It was the 1980s, the best and worst of times. In 1981, the bathhouse raids saw over three hundred gay men arrested, and thousands more demonstrating on the streets — the beginnings of Canada's Gay Liberation Movement. In 1984, Brian Mulroney was elected prime minister of Canada and would soon defund almost every women's, Indigenous and lesbian organization in the country. He also did his best to ignore the rising numbers of death notices with grainy photos of men in their twenties and thirties. By the end of the 1980s, over three thousand Canadians had died of AIDS.

Demonstration after demonstration. South Africa, Nicaragua. Abortion, AIDS, police violence. *Yes Means Yes, No Means No. Women United Will Never be Defeated. "El Pueblo Unido Jamás Será Vencido." US Out of El Salvador. Silence = Death.*

But the times then were more generous with rebellious artists like me: there were publishers, collectives and film societies where a broke feminist/lesbian/socialist artist in second-hand clothes could thrive. Despite Mulroney's best efforts, there were still government funding agencies that supported work critiquing the government. There were film and television institutions dedicated to women. You couldn't get rich, but you could spend most of your days making art, if you were willing to move around a lot and eat a quantity of rice and beans. I survived via a crazy quilt of jobs, including a gig as a production assistant in a Jell-O commercial. After being relegated to the kitchen to cut cubes of Jell-O into exact one-inch cubes, I quit and joined a feminist video collective.

In the 1980s, I moved a dozen times. Home was my friends, my art, my political involvements. And whatever shabby shared apartment I could make beautiful with rugs, pottery, feminist posters and the bohemian aromas of veggie stir-fry and brown rice. For the godless community of lesbians and artists in which I thrived, *Diet for a Small Planet* by Francis Moore Lappé was our gospel. Mollie Katzen, author of the hippie-ish *Moosewood Cookbook,* was our Julia Child. In those days, a meal comprised of vegetables and brown rice was political. Lappé argued that it was more sustainable to eat plant-based foods, rather than, say, beef, which uses up much more of the earth's resources. After reading her book, I never ate beef again.

Which was just as well, because all my extra money went to film stock and videotape, not food. My work — low budget video documentaries and experimental narratives — began to take off. Boarding pass in hand, I ran off to screening or reading gigs: an audience of one thousand at an LGBT film festival in San Francisco followed by an audience of one at a gay bookstore in New York. A night with new filmmaker friends amid the eighteenth-century arcades of Turin, Italy, drinking Negronis; a lonely night in a hotel room in Calgary, munching Doritos from the mini-bar. (Fun fact: I came out in Calgary, due to a well-meant poster describing me as a lesbian filmmaker. I decided: *OK why not.*)

My work bombed, or it was loved and appreciated. Either way, I never gave up.

But I couldn't escape my mother. Just as she had appeared at my graduation, she popped up in almost everything I wrote. Knowing my mother was there meant the roots were always there. What I now realize is that my mother was my muse. A muse is, typically, an artist's source of inspiration and the focus of the artist's work. The relationship between an artist and their muse can be transcendent, or it can be troubled. In my case, it was the latter, because my muse hadn't even agreed to the job.

A PLACE WITH TREES

For a while, I lived as though I did not have a family. There was no middle ground in those days: a single diasporic narrative on the one hand, a queer undoing of that story on the other. I kept a lot of things from my blood relatives, as most queers do. It wasn't secretiveness, exactly. It was a problem of translation. My parents didn't know that in 1983, I had co-founded a feminist video collective. That in 1985, on International Women's Day, hundreds of women occupied the Eaton's Department Store in Toronto in support of striking women retail workers, and that our collective made a documentary about it that screened across the country. As feminists, we wrote and published, furiously and prolifically, and we were heard: between 1970 and the late 1980s, there were over fifty feminist magazines and newspapers in Canada, and several women's presses.

"Write yourself. Your body must be heard," wrote French feminist Hélène Cixous in 1981, part of a movement to create a feminist literature that would be embodied, experimental, erotic. These ideas freed my writing. Coming from an old-world culture where pronouns were almost always plural, I delighted in the first person singular. I wrote and published personal essays with names like "From Homeplace to Displace" and "No Fixed Place to Be." In the latter essay, I wrote:

> For many lesbians... there is no possibility of return; the rhetoric of community as family displaces blood ties.

The bar, the community centre, the political movement, the circle of friends becomes a copy of a copy of "home."

I grieved the loss of blood family, and tracked it through my writing. Nothing could replace my mother's brusque familiarity and rough-hewn love, nor her food. But I could see no possibility for growth within the sheltering yet confining forest of family.

Still, loss can make you creative. I found a place with trees. I found a kindred older generation.

Haida was twenty years my senior, closer in age to my mother than to me. She was a respected Vancouver-based filmmaker and editor with a flamboyant personal style. She saw me do a book reading at a festival in Vancouver, somehow obtained my address, and sent me a long, hilarious and lyrical fan letter on thin blue airmail paper from Vietnam. She told me about her peripatetic life, half of it spent in Vancouver, the other half near Hanoi, where her partner lived. She told me about how life there "rolled slowly, like a childhood summer." She wrote about "yearning to become a space between the words, or even just a comma, in a Duras novel." She invited me to come visit anytime.

I arrived at YVR airport one damp fall evening in 1993, age thirty-four, with most of my belongings stuffed into two suitcases. Anyone else might have been horrified, but Haida took it all in stride. She found me at the luggage carousel, dashed toward me in her stylish Burberry raincoat and gave me a warm embrace. I noticed she had a bottle of wine under her arm, still in its liquor store bag. She drove me through the sparkling rain to her 1940s wood frame house, surrounded by trees, in the geographical centre of Vancouver. That first night, she fed me her trademark lamb moussaka in a kitchen full of books and wind-up toys. We drank Chardonnay late into the night, like long-lost friends.

I stayed in Haida's guest room for three months and ended up living in Vancouver for a decade. Perhaps I stayed because of Haida, for I became privy to the regular, raucous gatherings of local women filmmakers at her square kitchen table. As bottles of vodka and platters of crackers and cheese were passed around, as scarred egos got comforted and shy emerging filmmakers got mercilessly teased, I saw that family could have a variety of intriguing and irreverent meanings. With her husky smoker's voice and poetic worldview, Haida became a mentor, mother figure and friend to me until her death, twenty-five years later.

I met Jane Rule only once, but she also showed me a different way for family to be.

It was late December on the Strait of Georgia. Days of rain and mist cast the ocean, and the distant silhouette of mountains, into shades of silver and pewter. As our ferry approached Galiano Island, my friend Penny and I watched the colourful details of landscape emerge: chartreuse moss carpeting sandstone rocks; the bluish haze of cedar boughs.

A lanky man named Fred, in green work pants and plaid flannel shirt, was waiting for us in a beat-up old Dodge. He was there to drive us to Driftwood Cottages, and then to our luncheon destination. A soulful, damp greenness enveloped us as Fred drove across the bluffs of Galiano Island. While it's acceptable to ask for a pickup from the ferry, being chauffeured to someone's house for lunch was a little over the top. Unless, of course, you were going to Jane's.

Jane Rule — writer, anti-censorship activist, Canadian literary icon — was by then more or less retired. She lived in a rambling house she'd bought with her partner, Helen Sonthoff, thirty years earlier. Jane was as much a part of the backbone of the island as the dusky sandstone bluffs that form its ridge. She'd set up a low-interest system of lending money to island residents who couldn't get a bank loan. A film about her, *Fiction and Other Truths*, records how, in summer, island children would flock to her outdoor pool, where she and Helen acted as lifeguards and swimming instructors.

I had read Jane Rule's sixth novel, *The Young in One Another's Arms,* many years earlier. That book, about a diverse community of people living in a boarding house in Vancouver, run by tough, androgynous, fifty-year-old Ruth, gave me an image of family that made sense. It was a different way of being queer in the world. I imagined I'd someday move to Vancouver and live in a house much like Ruth's. The house didn't exist, of course, but it symbolized the polymorphous community I hoped to find.

The drive to Jane's wound along a road surrounded by fields and farmland, and then through rainforest, where a gilded light illuminated curling cedar branches draped with moss.

Fred asked Penny how she met Jane. She explained that they got to know each other when Penny published *Detained at Customs*, through Lazara, her micro-press. The chapbook documented Jane's testimony about censorship of LGBT books at the Little Sisters bookstore trial. They soon developed a routine of visits. Between visits, they exchanged letters. Jane always typed hers, composing them like small, exquisite essays. I have one myself, which she wrote to me after she'd read one of my books. "Our nouns are so different!" she wrote. "It's in naming that we give our worlds to each other." She ended with a kind of invitation: "I hope one day we might meet and have a chance to talk." When Penny told Jane we were coming up for a few days, she invited us both for lunch.

It's a bit intimidating to meet one of your very own literary icons. There she was, sitting regally in a chair overlooking the swimming pool. But as soon as she spoke, in her famously deep voice, I felt at home. Our nouns may have been different, but we had a shared vernacular of sexuality that spanned our generations. I suddenly got her in a way that wasn't about her writing or mine. I saw the authority and the vulnerability in her, coexisting without contradiction.

The living room was decorated in Danish Modern: you could relax easily in those low-slung dun-coloured chairs. Every so often, someone would drop by to deliver a late Christmas present or to ask if Jane needed help with this or that. This was as different a model for old age as any I'd ever seen.

Before our visit, Penny had sent Jane an article I'd written critiquing the struggle for same-sex marriage rights in Canada, and that got us talking.

Interesting article, said Jane gruffly, shifting in her chair to turn toward me. Her eyes glinted fiercely through horn-rimmed glasses, but her expression was kind.

Oh yeah, well. Thanks, I stuttered. *I mean, it's nothing you don't already know.*

Like me, Jane had long expressed her discomfort with the all-consuming struggle for same-sex marriage. In fact, I had quoted her in the article.

I was afraid to publish it, I continued. Same-sex marriage had just been legalized the year before. There'd been a flurry of weddings across the country. The normalcy I'd fled at such high cost was now taking root in my queer community. There was now this binary: coupled, or not.

But then reading Marx gave me courage, I said. *He felt that marriage damaged community.* Utopian thinker that he was, Marx believed that it was in community, not in private relationships, that true freedom existed.

There was a moment's silence. Perhaps I had overstepped. Who was I to spout Marxist theory to Jane Rule?

Jane pressed her hands against the chair arms. I thought she might be angry at me.

Exactly! she said, with indignation. *And it's also handing over power to the State. Hoping Daddy will take care of things. Well, yes, Daddy will, but not the way you'd like.*

Soon enough, it was time to eat. Jane had had arthritis for many years and now used a walker, but she ran her kitchen with cool authority, and produced a sensual, luscious meal to boot. The soup, a purée of wild mushrooms, stock and cream, was accented with sherry. It was accompanied by artisanal cheese from Salt Spring Island and pears from a friend's tree. Those pears oozed a sweet, ice-wine-like nectar that formed an amber pool on our dessert plates.

A thoughtful host, Jane put us at ease with her skills as a raconteur. As the wind and the rain blew across the cedars, we heard stories about her grandfather and his successive wives, quite the man about town. Helen got mentioned here and there: the complex Dutch pancakes she used to make, the way she'd organized the kitchen when they first arrived and how everything was still the same. Jane's voice, deep as it was, could hold sorrow and humour, like a chord. I could sense the softness and pleasure Helen had brought to her life, and I could see how she'd managed to keep those gifts alive.

It seemed to me that for Jane, all the pleasures of community did not make up for Helen's absence, but also that they weren't supposed to. After Helen died, Jane famously refused to apply for the survivor benefits she was entitled to under Canadian law. The way she and Helen saw it, being a couple was nothing to be rewarded for; it was how you made that relationship part of the world that counted. And that world was now completely, brutally changed, for it had a missing piece — Helen. But Jane's world was made of many pieces. There were neighbours and family members and ex-lovers; there were writers, and readers from all over the world.

We said goodbye as though we'd see one another again.

Jane died a year later, from a sudden, swift-moving cancer. The swimming pool she watched over had long since been emptied out. In one conversation with a friend, Jane likened it to an open grave. She was ready to go, even if those around her weren't ready for her to be gone.

Jane and Helen are buried together on Galiano Island, in a small graveyard, just past a sheep farm, on Cemetery Road. It is the same graveyard that appeared in *The Young In One Another's Arms*. Penny and I visited Jane's grave the last time we were on Galiano.

The plaque on Jane's grave reads: *Risk. Grow. Grieve.*

DAMAGE CONTROL

I'm at the airport. What's your address?
Mom? What?

My mother, on the phone. No *hello*, no *how are you*. She didn't believe the phone required such niceties.

I'm coming to stay for a few days. What's your address?

A year earlier, my mother had been diagnosed with cancer of the larynx. After twenty-four radiation treatments, the cancer was now in remission. She was travelling across the country to see her far-flung children. No doubt she'd had some reckoning with her own mortality. No doubt she was worried if she gave me more notice, I'd say no.

I gave my mom directions, hung up the phone and immediately started yanking posters off the walls, and photos off the fridge door. I planned to, metaphorically at least, return to the closet for the duration of my mom's visit.

The doorbell rang ferociously, and I ran down the narrow stairway of my flat to greet my mother. Grrrlfriend, my cat, got there first. I opened the door and Grrrlfriend did her usual welcoming, repetitive meowing. My mom kicked my cat aside, handed me her bags and strode upstairs.

I had been up all night working on a grant application for a new film, still in in my wrinkled T-shirt and sweatpants from the day before. I gave my mother my bedroom, promising to make up the bed after I'd done my laundry. My mother got settled and came into the kitchen, high-heeled shoes clacking on the linoleum.

I handed her a steaming mug of coffee.

What's all this? she said, hand gesturing imperiously to the kitchen table, covered in piles of paper and dirty cups.

I just finished a major grant application! I paused, waiting for an expression of congratulation.

When are you going to get a job?

Ma, this is *my job.*

Why didn't you become a journalist? You're such a good writer. You're wasting your talents! She sipped her coffee thoughtfully and added, *It's a sin.*

I went out and stood on my tiny fire escape, absorbing the news of my sinfulness.

That afternoon, I set about organizing and loading several weeks' worth of laundry onto the back of my bicycle. I secured a bulging garbage bag with bungee cords and headed to the laundromat four blocks away. When I returned, my mother was cleaning my stove. Back turned to me, scrubbing mercilessly, she said: *Don't think you're going to be riding that bike forever!*

But I love riding my bike. And it's great exercise, it's healthy, it doesn't pollute.

What about when you're in your forties? Your fifties? Your sixties!

I slipped out of the kitchen, feeling suddenly mortified about riding a bike.

I had no idea arthritis would someday make my mother's predictions come true. She was just trying to warn me, but perhaps she envied me as well. She had gone from dutiful daughter to wife in her twenties. She'd raised six children and helped her husband succeed in his academic career.

She'd never ridden a bicycle.

My mother was low energy and rather sullen during that visit. Nonetheless, on her second day there, I invited Haida and Penny for a salmon dinner. I wanted my mom to know me better, to know my community. She said she wasn't feeling well and stayed in her room. We had a desultory meal. Haida and Penny left early.

That night, as I scraped food from plates and fed scraps of leftover fish to my loudly purring cat, I wondered if it was time to have a frank conversation with my mom, if only as a form of damage control. My first book, *The Woman Who Loved Airports*, was about to be published. It was a thinly fictionalized collection of stories. My mother was in it. So was a succession of women lovers, and tales of breakups and loss. New to the autobiographical mode, it hadn't occurred to me to consult with my mother on her presence in my stories. There would be no book if I had.

I ran water for dishes, hands stirring the warm soapy water, too preoccupied to notice that the cat had jumped on the counter and had eaten an entire half filet of salmon.

I woke up early the next morning and put away the sleeping bag and the foam pad I'd been sleeping on in the living room. I made coffee and went to the bedroom with a cup for my mom. The door was open. She was getting dressed. I remember noticing how skinny and pale she was.

I placed the coffee on the bureau. *Mom.*

She was putting on pantyhose. She didn't turn around.

Mom. I'm a lesbian.

NO. It wasn't an exclamation. It was a firm rebuttal.

She grabbed a towel, wrapped it around herself and ran out of the room. Like a character in a slapstick comedy, I chased after her, shouting: *You can't even say the word, can you?*

My mother had locked herself in the bathroom.

I jiggled the doorknob. *Mom!* I was scared. *Mom?*

Silence. The sound of running water.

The door opening. Her face, wet with tears.

Yes I can! she exclaimed. *Lesbian! Lesbian! Lesbian!*

She slammed the bathroom door shut.

We left it at that. My mother knew. I could put the posters back up on the wall. Even so, I was disappointed. What did I expect? *I'm so glad you're a dyke! Let's have a party, with balloons and cake!*

It took me years to realize that this voluble, tragicomic response was my mother's first attempt at solidarity.

THE RAIN CAN BE BEAUTIFUL

The grass at the graveyard was brittle, almost brown, evidence of weeks of Alberta drought. It was hot, room-with-no-windows hot, prairie hot. Taras, Jeannie, Michael, Lydia and me. Just the five of us. It wasn't right. My younger brother's body headed for an oblong hole in the hard, dry Alberta ground. My youngest niece, Krystyna, the baby of the family, fifteen years old at the time, came up beside me, put her arm around me and pressed her head against mine. She held me like that, firmly and lovingly, and then we slowly walked away.

My younger brother, Roman, had moved to Vancouver and become a full-time street musician. He was beloved to commuters and tourists alike for his unorthodox combo of folkloric and pop music, played on an ancient harp-like instrument called the bandura.

    I lived in Vancouver, too. I was an artist, too. Rosemary Sullivan, in her book *Shadow Maker,* a biography of poet Gwendolyn MacEwen, describes the artists' existence in ominous terms: "The romantic notion of an artist as a solitary genius born with his or her eccentric talent is a brutal myth because it leaves artists essentially alone…It takes extraordinary stamina and luck for the artist to survive in modern culture. Art is not a safe profession."

    Roman and I had a shared avocation, but we didn't have much to do with each other. Every so often we'd go for coffee or I'd buy him a meal. I'd notice that his hands shook, that he loved books and booze, and that he talked about them like they were his best friends. Secretly, I judged him, like my mother had judged me. Why didn't he try to get a real job? I was unaware of the rich details of his life. Until he died from heart attack, or from poverty, or from trauma, at age forty-two. Inside his wallet was a wrinkled piece of paper with my name and phone number on it.

I spent a year atoning. Unreasonably, illogically, I thought I should have brought him food, clothes and gifts. I should have understood him. *I should have saved him.*

I produced an album of his songs. I interviewed his busker friends and made a radio documentary about the process of grieving my brother's death, called *Everything But Silence*, which aired on CBC. All over the dark, damp streets of Vancouver, I searched for Roman, tracing his footsteps along Granville Street, across Hastings and Main, down Blood Alley, past addicts pushing shopping carts, trying their best to stay alive, past the street corners where women had been picked up and never seen again, past the dark, musty pubs where Roman used to go to drink beer and read, past the hushed, expensive new restaurants, past the old Woodward's Department Store, where I'd volunteered at a squat to protest gentrification, years before.

I expected to see him, out of the corner of my eye, out of the blue, out of nowhere.

West Coast rain is powerful: the air turning to liquid, the colours an impressionist palette of blues and greys. You find your resolve melting, your initiative fading. It's fragrant and monotonous. If you're around it long enough, it changes you.

On days when the rain abated, I gathered up my courage, introduced myself to other buskers and asked them if they knew Roman. They all did. One guy, Dave, a scruffy guitar player with kind eyes, who uncannily resembled my brother, glanced sharply at me between songs and growled, *Stop beating yourself up. Roman wouldn't want that.*

The rain can be beautiful. The rain can test your patience. The rain can make you go over things you regret, make you forget the best parts of who you are.

Comfort came in the form of knowledge. Going through Roman's address book, I contacted a Ukrainian woman, Olenka, about the same age as Roman. She said they had been friends. Perhaps there'd been some romance. She had long orange hair, a round, sensuous body and the wary eyes of someone with a lot of secrets. Olenka told me she played the bandura too. She hung out with Roman while he performed, something he didn't usually allow, and sometimes jammed with him.

I met the kind, weathered people at Bullfrog, the recording studio where Roman produced his CDs. The Bullfrog folks let Roman record on credit. He'd bring them gifts, like ceramic figurines of angels, his totems. I went to the Carnegie Centre, a library and community centre, known as the living room of the Downtown Eastside. I found out that Roman went there frequently, to borrow books, or to eat a meal. They had a cafeteria with healthy food, run by volunteers. I ate a furtive lunch of lentil soup and spinach salad with balsamic dressing. It was delicious. It cost three dollars.

The knowledge was this: Roman didn't need to be saved.

Psychoanalysis was my penance, and my cure. Fifty minutes at a time in a damp basement room, my arms resting on the leather surface of a chair rubbed raw by twenty years' worth of patients. I could barely see what I was getting out of it, given how seldom my analyst spoke. How much I had to come up with on my own. Her basement office was low-ceilinged, with a narrow oblong of window. The art on her walls did not appeal. It was so unglamorous, so not *The Sopranos*. But I dragged my ass through snowstorms and bitter cold and pouring rain and dangerously high UV indexes to get to those dreary 9:30 a.m. sessions.

My father and grandmother had died a few years before Roman passed. I told the story of their deaths over and over and over. Each time from a different angle, until I had exhausted every last detail. Three deaths in five years. Funeral after funeral, in the same high-domed Ukrainian Catholic church covered in frescoes, an angry white-haired God glaring down at me. The unbearable loss of one's *own*, multiplied by the losses of diaspora.

My therapist, with her kind, narrow face, encouraged me to feel it all.

My dead brother weighed in, too. I was at home on a Friday night as usual, eating cheese, drinking wine and watching an entire third season of *The L Word*. A contract lecturer at three different universities, I worked seven days a week and had little time to make friends. In fact, I was quite proud of my ability to weather solitary weekends with a boxed set of entertainment and a ten-dollar bottle of wine. I had reached the grand finale of Season 3: preparations for a lesbian wedding in Whistler. All of my Marxist anti-marriage sensibilities were for naught. I was teary. Sobbing, really.

I was lonely too, said my brother.

Say what? I had only had a single glass of wine. But it was Friday night, I was exhausted from a week, a year, a decade of contract teaching. I was vulnerable, open to anything, even a conversation with a ghost.

But I had a community. I had my music. I had the bars. I had my neighbourhood.

OK so he really did want to argue this one out. Fine. *What about the drinking?* I asked wearily. Trying not to feel guilty about the opened bottle of wine on the coffee table. In fact, I poured myself another glass.

That was there. That was just part of who I was.

I'm so sorry, I whispered.

I wanted to discuss the loneliness thing too. How I'd finally figured out that we had shunned each other because we were so alike. The destructive Romantic notion of artist as social isolate that we'd grown up with. The razor-sharp shiver down my spine, whenever I saw him busking on the street. My brother, my mirror.

How we might have supported each other there.

But he was gone.

I stopped trying to get rid of sorrow. I just breathed it in.

Grief hung in the air like a damp veil of mist when I visited my family at Christmas that year. None of us could talk about Roman. I passed around things Michael and I found in his hotel room: sheets of music, a prayer book, some ceramic angels. Roman's bandura sat silently in my mother's living room, gathering dust.

On Christmas night, I listened to my mother crying herself to sleep.

A year after Roman's death, my mother's cancer reappeared. Her larynx and voice box had to be surgically removed. After the nine-hour surgery, she wept every day for three weeks. I know. I was there. I made soup, did her laundry, helped her wash herself, cajoled her into eating.

That was when my mother and I abandoned the ship that contained all of our grudges and hurts. That ship had been sturdy, powerful, never veering off course. I could recite the various maternal transgressions that were its cargo. But we jumped ship and we swam toward each other. It wasn't just me forgiving her, or vice versa. It wasn't an attempt at rescue. We started over again.

It's rare to have that happen with any relationship, let alone that between a mother and daughter, or an artist and her muse.

ICE CREAM

My mother was in her late seventies when her larynx was removed. She had to figure out how to talk, breathe and swallow, all over again. People would turn to stare when she spoke in a public place, for her voice was now deeply guttural, huskier than Lauren Bacall, deeper than Johnny Cash. They had no idea what a miracle of stubborn determination that voice was. *I liked her voice*, says Taras, unexpectedly, years after her death. *It had character.*

Many laryngectomy patients end up with a stomach tube. My mother refused this option, and worked constantly to improve her swallowing, learning to use her throat muscles in a new way. A lifelong foodie and gourmet cook, my mother would have to stick to soft and puréed foods for the rest of her life. Even so, eating was a laborious, noisy and often untidy business.

If my mother mourned any of this, she did so privately. She wore bright, patterned silk scarves to cover the hole in her throat, and pantsuits in lime green, or hot pink, to match. She'd stride into Eaton's, head directly to the makeup counter, and, in her Johnny Cash voice, ask about the latest Estée Lauder skin creams, ignoring the alarmed look of the cosmetologist. She kept cooking, even though she couldn't eat what she made, because cooking was her gift to the world. Lemon chicken. Rhubarb strawberry pie with streusel topping. *Medivnyk* (Ukrainian honey cake). Salmon *en papillote*.

Vera always dressed to the nines, even when attending Group. This was the laryngectomy support group she attended weekly for eight years, run by Leah, a warm-hearted ear-nose-throat specialist. Group's membership was 99 percent men in golf shirts and Edmonton Oilers baseball caps, the kind of working-class guys my mother had never had occasion to hang out with. They were in various stages of post-op recovery, some in wheelchairs with tubes coming out of their stomachs, others robust and confident, speaking into an electrolarynx — a microphone-like device that turns breath into speech. It's true they were all there to worship blonde, compassionate, miniskirted Leah. She made them talk, exclaimed over their vocalizing ability, gently scolded or excitedly praised them, hugged my mother as she managed to swallow liquids for the first time in a week. Mama outshone them all, even Leah said so. My mother was the Jackie Kennedy of the laryngectomy set.

Here, my mother could relax. She was with her own. She'd loosen her scarf, revealing the black hole in her throat. She'd sit back and smile as everyone, at Leah's urging, recounted where they were born.

My father had died several years earlier, of complications from cancer, at age seventy-three. My family went through a respectable mourning period, but his death had a strangely liberating effect on all of us. I began a Ph.D. at age forty-three. My mother bought a condo in Sidney, on Vancouver Island, and began travelling regularly between Sidney and Edmonton.

The only food that slid easily, smooth as silk, down my mother's narrowed-down esophagus, was ice cream. She couldn't get enough of it. I imagined it felt glamorous and glittery as it slid down. And so, my mother adored ice cream. She loved fancy ice cream and she loved crap ice cream. She was happy enough when I made her homemade dark-chocolate-with-sea-salt ice cream, or organic strawberry sorbet, but the huge cheap boxes of maple walnut ice cream from the frozen food section of Rexall Drugs were her staple. And ice cream bars were her secret vice.

Along with Taras and my sister Jeannie, I had become one of my mother's caregivers. I flew to Edmonton or Sidney regularly to shop and cook and accompany her to medical appointments.

One day, I came home after a trip to the organic grocery store. I had bags full of quinoa flakes, soya milk, miso and organic chicken broth. I had purchased yogurt and strawberries and bananas for smoothies, carrots and kale for juicing. All the time I was shopping, I thought carefully about providing Mama with different flavours and textures. I had pâté and hummus, cornmeal and cream cheese. My back hurt from lugging those groceries five blocks. I had easily spent a hundred bucks or more.

Here. Comes. Boot. Camp, muttered my mom. She was still in her PJs at 2 p.m., slippered feet on the coffee table, watching Gwyneth Paltrow on the *Rachael Ray Show* cooking chicken fajitas. I ignored her. Caregiving was hard work, and required, I found, not only patience but a small amount of impatience, as well.

I set to work unpacking groceries and peeling beets, carrots and ginger for her daily juice regime.

As I tossed scraps into the garbage, I noticed not one but two wooden ice cream sticks, with the remains of ice cream still on them, in the bin.

A fierce, sticky anger coagulated in my throat.

I confronted my mother. Voice shaking, I earnestly proclaimed all the ways I worked to get nutrition into her, making sure there would be good food in the fridge weeks after I'd left. I really got into it. What was the point of it all, I asked rhetorically, if she was eating garbage? When she ignored me I said, *OK that's it. I give up. Eat what you want.* I exited stage left, and went into the kitchen to clean up.

Gwyneth was loading the chicken into the gluten-free tortilla, saying, *It's so easy!*

My mother came into the kitchen. She stood there, in her favourite stained white nightgown with floral sprigs all over it, blue fuzzy slippers on her feet. She didn't have her dentures in, which made her look about 110 years old. There was a trace of chocolate around the edges of her mouth. *I'm. Sorry.* she said, in her raspy laryngectomy voice. *I'll. Try. Harder.*

OK, I said gruffly, and handed her the viscous brown liquid I'd just finished making. She took it and went back to her couch.

Years later, the friendly fire of my anger is the one thing I wish I could undo.

I tell my friend Marc about the ice cream episode, one afternoon while we're driving somewhere. Marc, a former chef, mulls over my mother's ice cream preference. *It's the mouthfeel,* she says. *The commercial ice cream felt better in her throat.*

My mother, in the last decade of her life, was choosing what *felt better.* She was solving the conundrum of pleasure, of making oneself happy amid difficult circumstances.

The idea compounds, stays with me like an ice cream headache. To choose pleasure: a skill I am only just starting to acquire.

BODY MEMORY

Recipes tell stories, bleed history, channel memory. They are their own cultural archive. My mother's Sweet-and-Sour Spare Ribs and her Jell-O Fruit Chiffon Cake are relics of a time long past.

Janet Theophano, author of *Eat My Words*, a social history of women's cookbooks, writes about finding an old, nineteenth-century journal in an antique shop. Upon closer inspection, she realized it was in fact a recipe collection, full of such varied lore as how to make Parker House Rolls or the best way to flush a colon. Newspaper clippings, devotional texts and, of course, recipes, filled its pages.

Women began to dominate the cookbook industry in the nineteenth century, and many of these cookbooks were community initiatives, like the church-sponsored recipe books to which my mother contributed. Those recipes are like scholarly texts, carefully tested and researched, and very territorial. The cake recipe you contributed was your original contribution to the field. Everyone expected to see my mom's Chocolate Rum Torte at weddings, anniversaries and funerals. You could say those recipes provided more comfort than any priestly sermon.

Theophano noticed that these early compilations were almost always written on recycled materials, like a husband's old shipping log or accounting ledger. Indeed, my mother's personal recipes are inscribed into a small, jade-green plastic-covered book, *Peking Review*, subtitled *Fiftieth Anniversary Gift Notebook*, scoffed from my father after they'd travelled to China sometime in the early sixties.

The book begins with an introduction to Maoist China, with phrases like "a century of heroic struggle" and "the big leap forward." At the end is a handy reference to Chinese dynasties and the Chinese phonetic alphabet. In between are a hundred or so blank pages, into which my mother inscribed her recipes, and sometimes phone numbers, too.

In her beautiful schoolgirl penmanship, Vera copied recipes as varied as Papaya Salmon Boats, Chicken Tetrazzini, and Hong's Egg Rolls on those tiny pages. Her recipe journal tracks food culture's orientalism in the 1960s, its Italianate turn in the early 1970s, and my mother's embrace of Vietnamese refugees and their food in the late 1970s, as large numbers of ethnic Chinese from Vietnam arrived in Canada.

We, her children, added to the recipe book. The very first recipe, for Slyvnyk, my mother's famous plum cake, is a palimpsest. It begins in my mother's handwriting but is overlaid with Jeannie's childish scrawl, added as my mother's writing began to fade. Halfway through the book, I recognize my printing: Stir-Fry Chicken. Terry's recipe. Delicious!!! (so he says!). The last recipes to be inscribed by my mother are shorter, the handwriting larger, messier. The final recipe in the book has only six ingredients, and no directions.

Good Marinade
⅓ cup oil
soya sauce
2 garlic cloves
1 Tbsp. rosemary
thyme
¼ cup brown sugar

Recipe books are possibly the oldest form of women's writing. But instead of giving directions for roasting meat or making bread, the earliest recipe books provided directions for magic. Theophano has uncovered papyrus relics from Egypt, written in Greek, Egyptian, Hebrew and Aramaic, that attest to a range of recipes for spells and healing potions. Later, as recipe books became more conventionally tied to culinary lore, herbal and magical remedies would often appear in the margins. Sometimes, as in my mother's Ukrainian Catholic Women's League cookbooks from the 1960s, fanciful concoctions, like "Recipe for Happiness," would appear at the ends of chapters, unconsciously echoing the supernatural tone of the earliest recipes ever written.

But I'd wager that most recipes go unrecorded; their residue exists as oral history, as body memory, as fragments of dreams. Baba's chicken stew recipe, for example, is not recorded in my mother's recipe journal: she would have watched her mother make it over and over again and would have internalized the proportions, the exact texture and taste it must have.

To write it down would have implied mortality, an end to oral history.

RECIPE FOR HAPPINESS

Into a large bowl pour a full cup of Thoughtfulness.
Add a generous helping of Friendship.
Mix in equal amounts of Generosity, Kindliness and Charity....

From Tested Recipes, *published by the Ukrainian Catholic Women's League of St. Josaphat's Parish, 1963.*

A lustrous, pearly winter morning in early December found me driven through somewhat treacherous Victoria streets by my seventy-nine-year-old mother. Vera had become a snowbird, spending her winters in Sidney. She still had a place in Edmonton, but she and Michael now time-shared a light-filled condo facing a marina. After twelve years of precarious labour as a sessional instructor, I finally snagged a full-time professor job at a university in Toronto. For the first time in my life, I basked uneasily in the glow of my mother's pride.

It had been an unusual, snowy December, and the roads, for residents who never have cause for snow tires, were dangerously icy. Still, the air smelled of ocean and cedar. Mama's coat was bright red, her scarf yellow and green. My battered grey suitcase was in the trunk. Just in from the airport, and already my mother was planning to show me off to her Ukrainian church lady friends.

By then I had spent many years of my life in big eastern cities. I carried that shameful secret that so many New Yorkers and Torontonians hold: I don't know how to drive.

As my mother executed a swift, smart U-turn, I craned my neck, looking fearfully in all directions. I curled up against the window, submitting to my mother's unruly ways of the road. Yellow lights; too slow, and then too fast; cars and pedestrians fleeing from her path. We had the whole day, but she had no time to spare. After all, she was about to turn eighty, and besides, this was the day of St. Mary's Ukrainian Catholic Church bazaar.

Even though I was in my forties, this relationship with my mother was new. We consciously *did stuff* together when I visited: The Rodin show at the Victoria Art Gallery, where my mother diligently watched a dour half-hour documentary on lost-wax casting. The fruit winery up the road, where Vera would lean against the tasting counter as though it was her local bar, tossing back doses of kiwi or blackberry wine like it was medicine. Foraging expeditions though the many thrift shops of Sidney, full-to-the-brim with the Blue Mountain ashtrays and perfumed cashmere sweaters of recently deceased seniors. Between excursions we'd sit in cafés and drink lattes, pensively gazing at the ocean.

What with the complications of speaking and the gravelly timbre of her voice, my mother's speech had become economic. Vera and I could no longer get tangled up in words, in the finely tuned methodology of pain that a mother and daughter can deploy. There was only this: my mother putting her finger to her throat, to plug its black hole, so that as she exhaled, air from her lungs made her prosthetic voice box vibrate, producing those *basso profundo* sounds. It took coordination, and resulted in judiciously chosen words, never more than five, or seven, or ten at a time. Mostly, my mother asked me questions, and I revelled in her attention, for she'd never inquired much before, afraid of what the answers might be. As for my mother's feelings or thoughts, I now had to search for them, in her cornflower blue eyes, the turn of her lips, the lightness or darkness of her expressive face, mobile as a mime's, and her marvellous, bright smile, which I hadn't seen for decades. She lived in the moment; she had to, and her appreciation of the smallest things was a life lesson. But mostly there was companionable silence, punctuated with stock gestures. The pointing/nodding that meant *I like that!*, the *A-OK* sign that resembled an Indian mudra, the diffident toss of the hand that meant she refused to endure one more sip of the green smoothie I'd made — were a rich vocabulary.

Emerging, with our lives intact, from the car and into the church basement, we were greeted with the nose-tingling smell of Baba's kitchen, the mingled aroma of cabbage, potatoes and garlic. While other Christmas fairs may feature everything garish, from home-sewn red and green table runners to squat ceramic Christmas trees, this one was no-shit serious: all about the food. I breathed a sigh of relief. The delicacies these women made, the smooth perogy dough they rolled out on worn Formica tables, the cabbage leaves they stuffed with brightly seasoned rice, and the desserts they made with expressive, purple-veined hands, were essential to my survival.

Most of the iron-armed, big-bosomed, lipsticked ladies who ran the bazaar had living memory of the old country, of war or of immigration. Their recollections are cluttered with camps and ships; their dreams feature lost shoes, murdered relatives and mad escapes through forests. If they didn't experience this, their parents or grandparents did, and the trauma seeps through the generations, a stain that won't go away.

Now they live in Victoria, and food is their compulsive return, their secret dialect, their recipe for happiness.

I could see the women laughing raucously behind tables laden with garlic sausage and fragrant, freshly made sauerkraut. I heard them passing on darkly fascinating anecdotes to one another while selling wheat berries, an essential ingredient for kutya, the signature dish of Ukrainian Christmas Eve.

My mother caught up on some gossip — who had cancer, who had died, what happened at the last perogy-making bee and some outrageous thing the new young priest had said in his sermon. She introduced me to Mrs. Semchuk and Mrs. Lewycky. *This. Is. My. Daughter. Marusya. She. Is. A. Professor.* She said that all the time now, a kind of incantation.

After suspiciously examining seemingly identical Ziploc baggies of wheat berries at different ladies' tables, my mother decided to buy some from Mrs. Krawchuk, and a mason jar of sauerkraut from Mrs. Melnyk. Then we sat at a card table covered in plastic gingham: I had apple pie, Ma had ice cream, of course, and we both sipped Red Rose tea.

We were pretty full, but Mama said, *We. Better. Get. Back. I. Made. That. Chicken. Stew. You. Like.*

My mother drove me slowly and gracefully back to her place in Sidney, a twenty-minute drive from Victoria. Snow sat lightly on green and brown pastures, like a light spill of flour.

The day ended with my mother's smooth, soft perogies, cradled in Baba's chicken stew. My mother sat across from me at the dining room table. There were blue fabric flowers in a crystal vase. A pile of bills at one end of the table. Some orange pill bottles at the other end. There was an embroidered table runner with a faded red stain.

Arms crossed, Vera watched with quiet satisfaction as I ate. She needed to see me eat as much as I needed to be fed.

I wondered when my mother first cooked this dish. Did any of Baba's stories come back to her, like the one about the train ride across Canada, or tales of demanding customers at the dry cleaner she ran? Perhaps Baba's recipe had become hers now. At some point, the ingredients, the amounts, the proper smells and textures would have become a kind of body memory.

This recipe like an old, frayed map I thought I'd lost.

This time, I remembered to ask my Ma what the ingredients were. This time, tempting mortality, I wrote them down.

FAMILY VALUES

This. Christmas. Might. Be. My. Last, my mother proclaimed sonorously over the phone, as early as October. Comfortably ensconced in my own life three thousand miles away, I gazed out at the turning leaves as she spoke. Perhaps I had a cocktail in hand. It's possible jazz was playing soulfully on the radio. *I. Want. You. To. Come,* she said in her ravaged voice. And then, the final, deadly, throaty: *Everyone. Will. Be. Here.*

Outside the windows of my apartment, there were children playing on the street. An elderly lady across the road, raking leaves, and indoors, Chet Baker's trumpet building to a crescendo. The details of the previous Christmas had long since faded from memory.

I said yes.

Three days after Christmas, I was still at my mother's condo in Edmonton. The teeming waves of relatives had finally receded, and I figured I'd be able to put in some quality time with my mother. Just me, her and the Weather Channel, which she watched with strict allegiance. She'd install herself on the couch, wads of Kleenex and a mixing bowl of maple walnut ice cream in front of her. She'd shout out the temperatures as though she was watching football.

Minus. Thirty. In. Ottawa!

Thirty-two. Above. In. Cairo!

It was her way of tracking her children's lives. That way, when they called, from Ontario, or Egypt, where Michael lived, she'd have a surefire conversation opener.

For the past three days we'd feasted: perogies, cabbage rolls, turkey, pickles, salad, mashed potatoes and gravy, fried fish, fruit compote, rugalach and poppyseed roll. The only things Vera could eat were the mashed potatoes and the puréed root vegetables I'd snuck onto the Christmas Day menu.

Once again, I trudged to the organic health food store. Spent the big bucks. Vegetables and fruits in every colour; soy milk, chicken broth, and yogurt for good measure. The total price could have bought us dinner in a fancy French restaurant, but I didn't care. This was going to make us feel better than *foie gras* ever could. For the rest of my stay, I was planning to make a half-dozen puréed soups that my mother could thaw later, after I'd gone.

I was putting the finishing touches on a cream of broccoli soup, and overhearing an in-depth analysis of weather systems in the American Midwest, when my mother came into the kitchen.

I. Just. Called. Everybody. They're. Coming. For. Soup.

I turned off the food processor.

Wait. What?

I. Sure. Hope. That. Soup. Will. Feed. Fifteen. People, she said, looking doubtfully at the food processor. She went back to the living room to catch the five o'clock *Weather Centre Live*, turning up the volume as she did so.

I gently lowered my head onto the kitchen counter. It was cool and quiet there. Thought about how, for three nights, I'd cleaned up after siblings, nieces, nephews, in-laws, uncles and strangers unrelated to me by blood or marriage, so my mother wouldn't be left with the job.

And then, I started watering down the soup.

Two hours later, my thin gruel was gone without a trace. The usual debris of dirty dishes, cutlery, bits of spilled or un-eaten food, greasy napkins and murky glassware covered the table, and the carpet as well. Taras asked if there was anything else to eat. *That soup was kind of watery,* he said. My mother rushed into the kitchen to prepare leftovers.

I threw on my coat and left.

I stood outside the condo building in the blistering cold. I wondered where exactly I thought I was going.

And then I remembered Woody's.

Years earlier, my mother had inadvertently moved into Edmonton's tiny gaybourhood. I'd always felt amused when we walked past the rainbow signs heralding a cluster of gay bars, a porn video/sex toy outlet and a steam bath.

It was time to rejoin my tribe.

I walked one block, climbed a set of dark, narrow stairs and sat down gingerly at the bar. There were only a few other patrons, mostly men, scattered throughout a dim space decorated with rainbow flags, gay beefcake photos and tinsel. I ordered a crantini, trying to look relaxed as I perched stiffly on my barstool. I looked over at the guy next to me: forty-some-thing, balding, dressed in a faded striped shirt and baggy jeans. He took a long gulp of beer, looked over at me and extended a large, weathered hand.

How d'ya do. Eric.

Eric's hand was sandpapery and warm. We clinked glasses. *You seem like you're in a bit of a hurry,* he said with an amused smile. I looked down and realized I hadn't yet taken off my coat. I removed it, smoothed it out on the stool next to me.

Visiting? asked Eric.

I'm from here, originally. Visiting my mother. She has a condo around the corner. I'm escaping Christmas.

Eric gave me a sad upside-down smile, like he'd seen it all before. *Welcome to Woody's,* he said, raising his glass. We settled in.

I told him about the three long days of TV, shopping malls and family dinners, nights tossing in a single bed on percale sheets. Talked about my mother's missing larynx. Described how, in the entire forty-eight hours I'd been there, no one had so much as asked me about the weather in Toronto, let alone about my relationship, my work or my writing.

While I was talking, Eric hailed the bartender with a practiced nod, and pointed at my empty martini glass. Then he crossed his arms, swivelled over to face me and said, *Here's the thing. Family's a relationship like any other. It's a process. Don't be so hard on yourself. Don't be so hard on them. You have to give it time. Doesn't work to be angry. Doesn't help.*

You sound like some kinda counsellor, I said. *You. Sound. Like. Dr. Phil.*

Turned out he was a counsellor, for at-risk youth. Uninvited by his own family, he'd had Christmas dinner at Woody's, an annual event.

If only I had known, I said.

We would have surely welcomed you, said Eric in his old-fashioned, ceremonious way.

Word spread quickly through the bar. A stranger, escaping a family Christmas. It was poignant, a made-for-TV Christmas movie. A group of Eric's friends ushered me outside for a toke. One of them, Rudy, tall, skinny, with bleached blonde hair, wounded puppy dog eyes and a pierced lip, told me he'd been kicked out of the house when his family found out he was gay. He was sixteen at the time. Moved into a homeless shelter. Been on his own ever since. Compared to his family, mine seemed like *The Brady Bunch.* But Rudy was empathetic, if not downright melodramatic: *I will personally pay your cab fare to the nearest lesbian bar.*

It was tempting, but I figured being out until 2 a.m. might worry my family. We went back inside. Rudy had to leave, but he introduced me to everyone, handed me a fresh crantini as he left and gave me a warm parting embrace. I joined a table of his friends reminiscing about the Christmas they'd just spent together in Mexico. I sat back and watched. There was a fifty-something bald guy with a beard and a single earring. There were two sporty middle-aged women with sensible shoes and identical haircuts, probably a couple. A guy with a ponytail, wearing a Duran Duran T-shirt. They'd obviously known one another for a while. But they paused every so often to explain bits of their conversation they thought I might not get. Occasionally, they asked me questions about my own life. Had I been to Mexico. How did I like Toronto.

At about midnight, I excused myself and slipped back to my mother's place. The dishes were where they'd been when I left, strewn across a stained tablecloth, and the entire family was gathered around the television watching a two-hour unedited recording of my niece's last dance performance. No one had noticed I was gone.

I quietly gathered the dirty dishes and stacked them in the dishwasher. Put detergent in, turned the machine on, went to brush my teeth.

I could hear my mother snoring and wheezing in the next room. From the living room came waves of laughter, *oohs* and *ahhs.* I knew that my family took care of my mother while I was away. That they saw my presence here as my turn, and that I wasn't supposed to mind. And I didn't, not really. It was the disinterest that rankled. *Doesn't work to be angry. Doesn't help. We would surely have welcomed you.* It was as though I had gone through a secret, temporary portal. Where I'd had a chance to see how bad and how good it can really get. I would always be split, neither here nor there. All I could do was get comfortable in that liminal space, with the secret knowledge I had of both worlds.

3

FOR MY MOTHER

It had taken me weeks. To make this phone call.

A Scotch on the rocks beside me, for courage. I was ready to hang up at any moment, should the need arise.

My mother's voice, deep and unworldly, came on the line. I could hear wind. And crackling electricity, and ocean.

We chatted. The weather. The grandchildren. World affairs. Her latest method for making really good chicken stock (use a crockpot). I gently brought the conversation to the issue at hand. My food memoir, *Comfort Food for Breakups: The Memoir of a Hungry Girl*, was about to go to press.

A question I needed to ask.

But first, I told my mother some funny stories about the advance publicity. The live phone interview on national radio. First time I spoke publicly for the book, me at my kitchen table, dressed in yoga pants, no bra, and an old feminist T-shirt that read "If I Can't Dance I Don't Want to Be Part of This Revolution." I held my cellphone close to my ear, waiting to go on air. I could hear the radio show going on in the background (behind them, that wind again). The hosts were chatting, lobbing witty repartee to each other, like the *pock pock pock* of a tennis ball:

Hey, didja ever go through a breakup and then all ya wanted to do was eat burgers and fries for a month?

For me it was ice cream. Every meal. For weeks.

Oh yeah? What flavour? Vanilla? Chocolate?...Rocky Road? (much laughter).

It was entirely possible that they had not read the book. The title, *Comfort Food for Breakups*, had been taken literally. What they wanted was self-help, or me listing the zany things I consumed after I got dumped. All I could think to do was to tell them an unfunny story about the time I stopped eating entirely.

That interview got heard by just about every single person I knew. Even by my childhood friend Nadia, who was driving home at night when my voice came on the radio. She told me this later: she stopped the car by the side of the road, and listened, in the dark.

Over the phone, I told Mama more stories. The long, dark conversation at Terroni with Marion, the food columnist from the *Toronto Star*. Like a 1940s newspaper woman with her vintage suit and her grand, brash manner. *Go ahead and order*, she'd said happily, in her plummy British accent, *It's on* The Star. It was the interview you always imagine: respectful, thoughtful, and even giggly at times. Over lightly grilled wild mushrooms dusted with parmesan, we talked about the Holocaust, and about her brother's soon-to-be published memoir that she was in. The ethical dilemmas of life writing. We talked about my book. Marion had savoured every single word.

My mother gasped, *tsk*ing in all the right places. We were both foodies now. We read *Gourmet* magazine like a detective novel, turning the pages hurriedly, impatiently. *Iron Chef* was our porn. When I visited we'd cook for each other (her: chicken stew with perogies; me: fried breaded oysters with mashed root vegetables). The food was a text, perhaps more of a hypertext. The food was a longstanding non-linear conversation.

I got to the point.

So, I've dedicated my book to you. Somehow it ended up coming out so furtively. Like I was admitting I stole from her purse when I was kid. (Which, I did.)

Really?

Yeah. I just wanted to make sure it's OK with you. I can still change it.

She was confused. Not sure what to say. Silence. Wind in the background, and then:

Oh.

I can take out your name. Nothing's final.

No. No. It's. Good. I'm. Honoured.

Now *I* wasn't sure what to say.

This was my fourth book. The first one caused quite a stir, to say the least. I keep an archive of letters I've received from readers over the years. Let's just say a couple of family missives didn't get filed — not the sort you like to reread. Let's just say my baba (grandmother), the love of my life, disowned me.

My second book, *Halfway to the East*, a volume of poetry, was much more benign. Through it, with it, I grieved the loss of Baba's love. But my mother, after reading it, said to me, rather grandly: *I. Am. Ashamed.*

My family didn't seem to know or care that I kept writing or publishing. That my books are in libraries. On people's bookshelves. On university course reading lists, and on Amazon.ca.

Alluvial deposits of memory / contain their voices / and traces of gesture / Baba's girlish laugh / her half-English, half-Ukrainian speech / the way my father always wore a hat / and kissed the ladies' hands.

For my eighty-one-year-old Catholic mother, born in a small village in western Ukraine, it had all been a bit of a stretch. Perhaps she wondered why I didn't write something *nice*. She'd been alternately embarrassed and diffident about my writing. We'd struggled with this for years.

The past few years, though, I'd started to read my stories to her.

While she was recovering from surgery. While I was visiting at Easter. At the end of a long day of cooking and serving food. Her feet up on the coffee table, bowl of ice cream on her lap. Stories about food, stories about ex-lovers. About the old country, about travelling, about family, blood and not. My stories, her stories. The same, and different.

I had stopped expecting anything from her.

Maybe, she said over the phone, her voice sounding dutiful, the good Catholic girl: *Maybe. You. Should. Dedicate. It. To. Baba.*

Yeah, no. I already did. My first book – I don't think you read it.

Oh. OK. She sounded relieved.

So. I took a deep and jagged breath. *You're going to love some stuff in the book, and then there's stuff you won't love as much.* (I hadn't read her everything.) Now *I* sounded like a schoolgirl. You'd never imagine I had a Ph.D.

Well. Of. Course, she said. *That's. How. It. Is. Every. Book's. Like. That.*

She had a bachelor's degree in French literature. Got it when she was in her forties. She was finally getting to use it.

But also, I said, still the earnest teenager, eager to please, *There's a lot of Tato* (father) *in it. I think you'll like that.*

What. Does. He. Have. To. Do. With. Anything? she said. Voice swelling a little bit in indignation.

I couldn't help but burst out laughing. She'd taken ownership. The book was hers now.

Or, perhaps more to the point: it was ours.

BRINGING BACK MEMORY

It brought back memories, said my youngest sister, Lydia, with a sigh.

We were walking around my mother's neighbourhood, grabbing an illicit smoke on a starlit Christmas Eve, snow like icing sugar dusting our coats. She said it quietly, with innocent gravitas. She was talking about my new book. She didn't say which memories, and she didn't say if they were good memories or bad.

In fact, I'd heard this phrase from almost every member of my family: *it brought back memories.*

My mother and father had brought nothing from the old country. Not candlesticks, not rugs. Not even a tattered Bible or a treasured *Kobzar* (a collection of poetry by Taras Shevchenko). No photographs or documents from before the 1950s. No worn metal chest, no tattered suitcase bearing the sticker of the Cunard Steamship Line.

This was not a trip that called for memorabilia. And how could you possibly hold onto anything during that journey. Except your own body and soul, and even those did not emerge whole.

I once asked my mother, *What is your earliest memory?* I had hoped for some texture, some colour, images of early twentieth-century Ukraine.

I. Remember. My. Tato. Going. Away. To. Canada. I. Remember. How. Much. I. Missed. Him, was all she said.

There *were* memories, in uneven tatters. A very short story, told and retold by Baba, of arriving by train from Montreal to Winnipeg, after arriving by ship from Hamburg. Flat broke, with two small children tugging hungrily at her sleeve, she asked a cousin, who met them at the train station, for money. Just a dollar or two (this must have felt like disgrace). He put his hands inside his pockets, pulled out a handful of buttons. It was 1932.

For my father, a concentration camp and then a displaced person's camp. Occasional hushed mentions of deportations, slave labour and mass graves.

And so, almost no family archive, oral or written. I had grown accustomed to my short history. Much like my father, who, since I was small, had felt death to be around the corner, I visualized a correspondingly short future. As though our lives had been cut out of larger cloth, extra material long since tossed away. Nothing left, ever. To make adjustments with, to patch holes, to extend, or expand.

For what it was worth, I had written a few things down. My family didn't seem to mind. Maybe they understood my book as a kind of archive. Archives, as French philosopher Jacques Derrida has pointed out, are surprisingly selective. But it gives you a kind of security. Knowing the archive is there.

My family accepted my book, grudgingly, at first. Then curiously, and finally with graciousness. Like a new member of the family they hadn't expected, but thought they could grow to love.

In Edmonton, first stop on my western Canada book tour, I was met at the airport by my mother and my older sister,

Jeannie, whom I hadn't spoken to in some time. *I read your book three times*, said Jeannie, with a frown. As though the compelling nature of my memoir had been something of an imposition. But then, to clarify, *I actually highlighted the parts I liked.*

I counted six family members at my reading the next night at Audrey's Bookstore on Jasper Avenue, among the strangers and friends. Jeannie was there, with a smug smile, like a VIP with a backstage pass. Three nieces — Sonya, Kryssy and Natalie — showed up, wearing pretty dresses: they sat together and giggled nervously. Taras came and hung out on the sidelines, hands in pockets, jiggling change. My mother brought a tray of her baking, precaution against whatever store-bought cookies the bookstore might provide. She sat in the front row, dressed beautifully: gold brocade jacket and a long black skirt, white hair gleaming. In the row behind her sat her friend Sonya (we called her Big Sonya), grey hairdo poufed to perfection. Arms crossed. Mouth set in a grim red line.

I was dawdling, waiting for friends to arrive. But my mother, taking charge (the book was dedicated to *her*, after all), ordered me to start.

Just as I began, a gang of queer women from the university clacked down the stairs in their flashy print dresses, tattoos, baggy jeans, Fluevogs and high heels. They had goofy, apologetic smiles on their faces. My mother frowned at them. They filled the last row, a protective margin.

It was terrifying reading to that crowd. I had taken precautions, emailing the major characters in the book the relevant passages. Still, I anticipated all manner of difficulty. I had transcribed their lives, at least the edges that overlapped with mine. There were bound to be some border wars.

During the time that I was writing the book: an odd, unsettling dream.

The cover page of my food memoir gets caught in the furnace of my mother's house, setting it on fire. I try desperately to rescue my family. My youngest sister comes running toward my open arms, but then runs past me, and perishes. The only survivors are two distant relatives, whom I hardly know. I survive the fire. My book, dangerous and all-powerful, kills my entire immediate family.

I was staying at my mother's at the time. I told her about the dream. She shrugged nonchalantly, and put some rye bread in the toaster. As I made her some carrot-apple-beet juice, she told me what she had dreamt.

I. Dreamed. I. Was. Getting. Married. Again. I. Had. Met. This. Guy. I. Didn't. Know. Him. Very. Well. But. He. Seemed. Nice.

I laughed out loud. My mom's unconscious, so loose and free! And this amiable guy, about to do a trip down the aisle with my mother.

My own dream stayed with me, left an almost invisible stain. I rewrote the final draft carefully, too carefully. What would my family think? How would friends and various exes react? And what about the Divas of the Church? That was the name I gave to my mother, Big Sonya and their friends: notorious high-femme Ukrainian ladies. I'd written about them, too. Would I never eat their homemade cherry squares again?

Memoir, like memory, is an incomplete document. It records, but it also invents: dialogue, description, exposition. It also notes absences: what wasn't said, or could have been said. Memoir is highly interactive. Its subjects will argue, and add to your story long after it's been published. *Baba had an electric stove, not a gas stove,* wrote Taras in an email, after I sent him a chapter from the book. *She was born in 1906, not 1903. Tato's brother was named Taras, not Mikhailo. I was named after him.* After submitting this errata sheet (which I publish, finally, here), my brother was fully onside.

I was amazed. That their disagreements were about details. Not about tone, or point-of-view, nor even about my right to tell these stories.

During the reading, I kept glancing at Big Sonya. Her expression hadn't shifted for the entire reading. This worried me. Big Sonya usually cried at any event, major or minor.

From her front row command post, Ma gave me the windup sign, universal code for "it's time to stop."

I read the final story. I looked up, caught Big Sonya ostentatiously wiping away a tear.

RETURN

We'd met online. Coincidentally, we both worked at the same university. We'd been dating for five months, having a companionable, good-humoured and slightly awkward time of it. We went to movies, cooked dinner together and took walks on the beach. This was the untroubled and slightly boring relationship I'd been wanting for quite some time.

Gwen had two kids. She had never lived alone, had barely travelled. She liked plain food, nothing spicy, and disliked jazz. But she had a wide comic-book smile and great posture. We laughed often, about silly things. I felt my heart opening, just a little bit.

It so happened we were planning to be in Edmonton at the same time. I was staying at my mother's and Gwen was visiting her best friend Rona. What luck, I thought, that these two places were only a half-hour walk apart.

And so, I allowed myself a detailed fantasy. I'd show Gwen my childhood landmarks, from the shabby little stucco bungalow of my earliest years, to the cheesy Storyland Valley Zoo peopled with nursery rhyme characters. I'd even bestow on her the greatest honour of East European culture; I'd take her to the graveyard and show her the final resting place of all my dead.

But as soon as I arrived in my hometown, I started shrinking in size. Gwen was arriving the next day. Without a partner, I felt like a large child.

My mother greeted me with her frail, hopeful embrace and her welcoming meal: perogies and Baba's chicken stew. Taras and his son Stephan joined us. We all feasted, gratefully.

Children have an instinctive sensitivity to injustice, and in my large-child state, so did I. I noticed that the dinner conversation focused on my brother and his son. It seemed that my mother basked in the reflected glory of their significant but quite ordinary masculinity, as well as its evolution. Like most women of her generation, my mother considered men's ability to raise children, or keep house, to be quite miraculous. After he'd finished eating, Taras got up and put his dish in the dishwasher. *Look. He's. Putting. His. Dish. Away,* said Vera fondly.

I told myself that I had been in exile, and had now returned. I felt very noble as I thought this, like a dissident writer.

I had reconciled with my mother and brother: they were now allies, more or less. But families can be a kind of time warp, an involuntary return to trauma. Within a few days, I was conversing at a Grade 4 level. My adult life, with all of its recently added on grown-up features — job, mortgage, partner — seemed unrecognizable to my family.

One afternoon, my mother told me about my niece and her "nice" boyfriend (who, it turns out, is a flaming queer). *Well, I have a nice girlfriend,* I blurted out clumsily, truculently.

My mother, too, had reverted. She was now the mother of a ten-year-old: *You. Should. Have. A. Boyfriend. Not. A. Girlfriend.*

With exquisite timing, it was this moment I chose to announce Gwen's presence in Edmonton: *She's staying at her friend's place. It's nearby. I want you to meet her. I want us to have dinner together.*

My mother's face reddened, tightened. She turned up the volume on the TV.

Did you hear me? I said, my voice shrill.

I. Can't. Discuss. This. Right. Now.

I called Gwen. She was having cocktails with Rona and Rona's partner, Ellie. In the background, I could hear clinking glasses, laughter and Drake. From my shrunken perspective, this seemed unbelievably sophisticated. I couldn't believe my misfortune in being here at my mother's, amid 1980s floral couches and back-to-back reruns of *Say Yes to the Dress*.

I told Gwen what had just happened. I told her I needed to see her.

I'm sorry you're feeling bad, she said warily. *I'm sorry I can't be there for you.*

The next day, Gwen and I met for coffee at a Starbucks exactly halfway between her place and mine. The distance between us had doubled, tripled. I had shrunk even more.

How are you feeling? asked Gwen, uneasily.

I'm going crazy! You have no idea! I'm invisible to them! I'm just a cook, a bottle washer, a handmaid —

My bag was ringing. I yanked out my cellphone. No one ever calls me in Edmonton. I couldn't imagine who it might be.

It was my mother.

Bring. Her. Now. I. Want. To. Meet. Her.

TEA PARTY

Gwen didn't blink an eye when I put down my cellphone. *That was my mom. She wants you to come for tea.*

OK, said Gwen, already standing and putting on her leather jacket. She took a deep breath: *Let's do this.*

She seemed heroic in that moment, a fighter pilot ready for battle. We walked over to my mom's condo.

My mother had brought out the fancy china teacups, covered with pink and yellow cabbage roses. She had put on a nice red blouse, and had arranged some of her baking on a plate. There was poppyseed roll, honey cake and rugaleh. The good silver, too. But it was tea, not dinner, and we were in the kitchen, not the dining room. The Weather Channel cooed softly in the background. There were limits.

Gwen and my mother shook hands, stiffly, like a senior and a junior diplomat meeting to do trade talks.

We all sat ourselves down at the kitchen table, quite carefully. I was having an out-of-body experience. I worried that Gwen would be overwhelmed by the embroidery, the pastries, my mother's sepulchural vocalizations, the hole in her throat.

But Gwen knew exactly what to do. She asked after my mother's health, complimented her on her baking. I chewed my poppyseed roll like it was a full-time job.

It felt to me like the world had tilted, slightly, and I couldn't get my footing. Who was I, if I wasn't invisible?

I could hear them talking, but their voices sounded watery, and far away.

We. Lived. In. Ottawa. Before. My mother was saying. *It. Is. A. Beautiful. City. I. Liked. It. There.*

Was it hard for you to leave? asked Gwen, with her curious squint.

Yes. It. Was, sighed my mother. *It. Really. Was.*

I'd never really understood my mother as someone with likes and dislikes. It always seemed to me that she floated gracefully along with my father's career changes, the perfect faculty wife. My father's death was just another one of those career changes.

It had been her decision to move back to Edmonton, I thought. My brother and sister were there, and old friends, and the church she'd married in.

She sold the Ottawa house she'd lived in for twenty-some years. Sold it herself, with no real estate agent, then started to have yard sales every weekend, selling off the family memorabilia. I chanced upon one of those bleak events one weekend when I was visiting. My sister Lydia stood sadly behind a table loaded with china figurines, a Seattle Space Needle ashtray, my father's Super 8 projector and just about every single painting and sketch I'd ever gifted my parents. All of our precious stuff, displayed for the neighbours, a museum of trivia and aspiration. My mother had seemed quite pragmatic and unsentimental about the move.

It never once occurred to me to ask her how she felt about having to move from a place she loved so that there'd be someone to take care of her in her old age.

I tuned back into the conversation. Gwen was telling my mother about her own children, two sons, now in their twenties. How they'd gone to French Immersion. How she had mixed feelings about it now. If my mother was surprised that a fifty-something lesbian had children, let alone queer spawn who spoke French, she hid it with admirable aplomb. Mama talked about learning French from the nuns in Morinville, where she grew up. How she used to hang out there on weekends. She repeated the phrase we'd heard so often as children: *That. Convent. Was. Like. Heaven. For. Me.* She told Gwen about getting her B.A. in Quebecois literature, in her forties (at a time when Quebecois literature was not at all in vogue). How she'd had to interrupt her studies to have Lydia, my youngest sibling. This was something I'd forgotten. The determination it must have taken to finish that degree, with a toddler in the house. Her sixth child.

Your children have done very well, Gwen said, gravely.

My mother blushed. *Oh. I. Don't. Know,* she said.

But it was the one thing she most wanted to hear. Not just from my girlfriend. From anyone. Her children doing well was her legacy, her autobiography.

The tea party slash diplomatic summit lasted all of twenty minutes, and then we left.

Wow, that was huge, I said to Gwen. *You were great.*

She's an interesting woman, said Gwen slowly. *Tough. Really smart. Doesn't miss a thing.*

I couldn't believe how many things I'd missed, over the years.

THE KEY OF SARCASM

My Facebook friend Isabel regularly posts comments like the following in her feed:

What's on your mind?

Emergency Meeting of Misunderstood Sarcastic People Support Group. My house, 8 a.m.

I have joined her fake group and clicked on Like countless times, for I am frequently misunderstood for my sarcasm.

But not by my mother. Vera had a great, unheralded talent for caustic comebacks.

Sarcasm requires a certain skill set: acting ability, a sense of timing and intonation. My mom rocked all of that, but her intonation was especially impressive, given that she did not have vocal chords. Her voice was husky, mostly one note. But if she was so moved, say, by a bad movie or a particularly idiotic medical practitioner, she could hit all the right notes in the key of sarcasm.

I'd say to her, over her iconic perogies and chicken stew, *CBC News* in the background, *I think I'm going to quit my job.*

My job was an ache in my back, a groan in my stomach, a headache in the night.

Silence from my mother. She'd been an academic's wife for forty years. One of the meanings of academic is, "a person who is academic in background, attitudes, methods, etc." The academy was a kind of home for her. My tenured academic job was her dream come true. As far as she was concerned, we finally had something in common.

I think I'm going to open a churrasco chicken joint in the east end. Do you realize there are no churrasco chicken places in my neighbourhood? I'm going to call it Dr. Chicken, Ph.D.

The slightest exhalation of breath, over at the fridge, where Ma was pulling out her poppyseed roll for dessert.

What. A. Great. Idea, she said.

One of my mom's favourite phrases, handed down by her mother, was the Ukrainian aphorism, "*Starist ne radist.*" Literal translation: "Old age is not joy."

Vera said it to me one morning when I was visiting. She felt like crap, her food wasn't going down, she had diarrhea. Life pretty much sucked, that day. *Starist. Ne. Radist,* she sighed. I said, *Oh c'mon. There must be some positive things to being old. Can't you think of any?*

She didn't mock me, or leave the room. She pretended to ponder my rather disingenuous question. She glanced out the window, at the boats and the water. She looked back at me with a flat expression.

No. Fees. At. The. Bank, was all she said.

ROAD TRIP

There's a story, *Love You Forever*, by Robert Munsch, about the life cycle of a mother and child. In short, the story begins with the mother cradling the child, and it ends with the child cradling the elderly mother, singing:

I'll love you forever,
I'll like you for always,
As long as I'm living
My Mommy you'll be.

It was never that simple, with me and my mom.

On one visit, I was more aware of my mother's increasing frailty. How gingerly she moved when we went for a walk along Tsehum Harbour, like someone walking against a wind. How sparse her speech: entire afternoons now thick with silence, a return of that grey maternal hush I remembered so uncomfortably from childhood. The number of naps she took: five or six in one day, sitting on the couch, head bobbing down into the relief of sleep. My mother was now, I realized, a citizen in the land of the very old. I was a foreigner there. I felt helpless, scared. Who would I be without a mother?

I camouflaged my fears with officious, parental behaviour.

Ma, why don't we go for a walk, you'll feel better.

Mom, how about I sign you up for seniors' carpet bowling?

Mama, what d'you think about Arthritis Aquafit?

Vera had never been a joiner. She waited me out.

Then came the day she casually proposed a day trip, to Point No Point restaurant, just outside of Sooke. I glanced at the map. It seemed easy enough.

(This might be a good time to remind the reader that I do not drive.)

I sat in the passenger seat as my mother huddled over the wheel. Fields, towns and hills flew past us. Cedar spires of blue and green. A wavering yellow line, solid or dashed, leading us away from medicine bottles and calendars filled with doctors' appointments. Glimpses of blue horizon, making us feel dreamy, and hopeful.

The drive was longer than I'd thought, but we got there without incident, just as a soft rain, no more than a mist, really, began to fall. We were seated in a light-filled room full of windows overlooking the Juan de Fuca Straight, waves unfurling against black shiny rocks down below. There were binoculars on the table. Vera held them to her face with her skinny, bony hands. She looked like an explorer, or a detective.

My mother ordered potato-leek-chicken soup with paprika oil. I had a shellfish stew and a local dry rosé. A weight fell off my shoulders. For a moment, my mother and I were equals, companions in all manner of culinary adventure. Who else would drive one and a half hours for lunch?

Dessert, a luscious chocolate mousse, was her reward. My mother took a mouthful, closed her eyes and shivered with delight. To witness her living in the moment, to see such deep pleasure amid suffering, was *my* reward.

The bill arrived, and my mother grabbed it forcefully, like she always did. We gathered our things, regretfully. My mother got us back on the narrow Sooke Road, and then it began to rain in earnest.

The highway became a coiling blue satin ribbon. The windshield blurred, cleared and then blurred again, as though we had Vaseline on our glasses and couldn't wipe it away. My mother held steady at fifty kilometres per hour, some twenty kph slower than anyone else on the road. A car behind us, trapped in a no-passing zone, honked aggressively. I looked over at my driver: no expression, her face a mask of Zen-like calm.

There were granite cliffs on one side of the road, splattered with chartreuse moss. On the other side, glimpses of grey ocean, boiling furiously.

When we stopped for coffee in Sooke, I noticed that her hands were shaking.

We (or rather she) kept driving. The rain got heavier.

I was a child again. I was a schoolgirl; my mother was driving me home from piano lessons, from Ukrainian Girl Scouts, from Ukrainian School. Mama had always been silent on those drives (as she was now), and I had always felt guilty — for needing her, for wanting not to need.

My mother was determined to get us home. The normal order of things had reasserted itself. She was the parent, the hero, the one who would protect us and keep us safe.

She was the one who would get us home.

Back on Highway 17, on the final stretch to Sidney, the sun came out. I asked my mother how she felt.

It. Was. A Good. Experience, she said. *To. See. That. I. Could. Do. It. After. All. I'm. Eighty. One. Years. Old.*

4.

CUBA

The in-flight movie has ended. We've been told by the flight attendant to lift our window blinds.

I see the blue skin of ocean. I see the end of a peninsula, like a faint scratch in flesh. A boat bisects the water, its wake like a spine.

The plane lowers, and green farm fields appear, and vintage cars parked here and there. A rural landscape from the 1950s, part fairytale and part tragedy.

We have arrived in Cuba. The passengers break into applause.

We wept when we encountered each other in the tiny Juan Gualberto Gomez Airport in Varadero. I had arrived in Cuba from Toronto, she from Vancouver. My mother looked so tiny and ladylike in her tidy white pantsuit, floral scarf and perfectly-set white candy-floss hair. We had been planning this trip for a year. I was feeling daunted by 150 midterm papers and the demands of my university job. But my mother had just turned eighty-two, and there was no putting things off.

After we got through Customs, I grabbed my mother's rolling suitcase, along with my own, and shepherded us through a parking lot steaming with diesel fumes, to the hotel bus. The air was a damp, warm blanket of humidity. The bus drove us along the edge of the ocean, plumes of white froth rising against rocky shores.

We could see hardscrabble villages of pink and yellow cinderblock, complex networks of clotheslines flapping in the breeze. Chickens strolled casually to and fro, barefoot children ran about, and an occasional skinny cow grazed by the road. It was jarring how there were no fast food places, no neon signs for Arby's or McDonald's, no billboards, except for hand-painted signs enumerating the benefits of the revolution.

Esteban, our sardonic tour guide (every hotel bus has one) gave us a kind of orientation. He told us where to get the best cigars and rum, what Cubans made per month (twenty to thirty dollars at the time) and the problems created by the double currency — one for tourists (Cuban Convertible Pesos) and one for Cubans (Cuban Pesos) — which has created something of a class society in a socialist country. Esteban continued, while the Canadian tourists mostly ignored him, fiddling with iPods or pointing at the vintage cars passing by. *Many of the waiters and maids you will see at your hotel,* he said, gazing wearily into middle distance, *are lawyers, teachers and economists. They can make more with tips from Convertible Pesos than they ever will in their professional jobs.*

Myself, I am professor of linguistics, Esteban informed us, and then, drily, sadly, said, *Don't forget to tip as you leave the bus.*

"Revolution is strong medicine," wrote Jean-Paul Sartre, about Cuba. "A society breaks its bones with hammer blows, demolishes its structures, overthrows its institutions, transforms the regime of property and redistributes its wealth [...] and, in the very moment of its most radical destruction, seeks to reconstruct, to give itself by bone grafts a new skeleton."

It was 2010, over forty years since Sartre had written that passage. But like any of the post-Soviet countries we'd visited, both my mother and I could see that this was still a culture of scars and contradictions. *This. Reminds. Me. Of. Ukraine*, she whispered, so Esteban wouldn't hear.

We arrived at our hotel and filed off the bus, clumsily pulling Convertible Pesos for the driver and tour guide out of our pockets. As I waited for our luggage to appear, I looked around me. We had landed in a pristine compound of candy-coloured buildings surrounded by lush gardens. Canadian vacationers (we are still Cuba's biggest tourist market) strolled about in plaid shorts from Mark's Work Warehouse, sundresses from Winners. We could hear Newfoundland accents, Québécois *joual* and the broad vowels of prairie speech. It seemed we had travelled so far only to find ourselves at home.

There was a slight mocking tone to the voices of the tourists. I could overhear them complaining about the airport tax and the food in the buffet. They were laughing at the outdated cars.

I felt smugly superior. As a young art student, I had devoured the vibrant cinema of the *Instituto Cubano del Arte e Industria Cinematográficos*, Cuba's revolutionary national film board. Those films had opened my eyes to the feminist achievements of the revolution, juxtaposed against everyday sexism and machismo. All-woman platoons had fought alongside Che and Fidel during the revolution. Universal daycare for working women was one of the Cuban revolution's most admired achievements, an issue in which Canada still lags far behind.

And here I was in a gated compound, all the Mojitos I could drink available at the bar, banana palms swaying diffidently in a gentle breeze.

When we got to our room, I sat outside on the tiny terrace while my mother napped. Warm Caribbean air caressed my skin. I could hear Vera's light, precise snores. A Cuban man tended the already immaculate lawn. The foreign-language chorus of birds, and the incense of ocean and flowers, were incredible to a Canadian delivered from the jaws of winter. This was the first time I'd done anything like this with my mother. We'd long since reconciled, but a week together on a package-deal vacation may have been pushing it. Especially in a place rumoured to have lousy food.

Soon enough, my mother and I fell into a sleepy, relaxing routine. I usually woke first, to the delicate sepia filigree of light coming in from the patio. I'd get dressed, write a note for my ma and emerge into luscious Caribbean colour: purple and pink bougainvillea, the lime green tracery of palms, a pale blue sky. I'd walk slowly to the hotel bar, savouring the citrus scent of the air. *Uno cappuccino por favor.* Cuban coffee: thick, sweet and bitter. I'd sidestep my fellow Canadians ordering piña coladas at eight in the morning, sit on the patio, sip my coffee and watch the lemon light turn to deep gold.

After a leisurely breakfast, my mother and I headed to the beach. Vera carefully lowered herself into a lounge chair, staying there for hours, reading magazines or giggling at tourists falling off banana boats. At regular intervals I brought her piña coladas, which she accepted as gravely as though they were heart medicine.

One day, over lunch in the compound's faux Italian restaurant with its faux pizza and pasta and its never-available tiramisu, my mother looked at me slyly and said, *There's. Something. I. Want. To. Ask. You.* There was a combination of innocence and craftiness in her watery blue eyes.

My thoughts turned immediately to my finances. How much had she picked up on? Did she know about the unpaid back taxes? The maxed-out credit card? Had she intuited that I'm like one of those people that appear on Dr. Phil, bewildered, wild-eyed, the audience glaring in disbelief as the good doctor lists on a screen behind him how much money has been paid in interest payments alone?

My mother's gaze wandered briefly around the room, taking in the birds flying in slow, confused arcs across the arched ceilings of the restaurant. Then she turned back to me.

Why, she said and then faltered. *Why. Haven't. You. Been. Talking. About. Gwen?*

I told my mother we'd broken up. To my alarm, she wanted to know why.

Taking a swig of sparkling wine, I told her my elaborate theory of why Gwen had left me. The trauma of her brother's N-stage cancer, Gwen's abusive childhood, the former triggering memories of the latter.

My mother nodded, sympathetically it seemed, and then said, with a small frown, *You. Know. I. Had. A. Funny. Feeling. About. Her.*

I changed the subject immediately. I worried my mother was being homophobic, in her inimitably indirect way.

But later, sitting on the patio while my mother napped, I realized she was taking sides.

She was taking *my* side.

The days passed slowly, a blur of repeating frames. Like the lens of a camera, I reverted to close-up. The contradictions and ironies of our Cuban tourism mostly fell away from my mind's focus. My mother's nutritional needs (she had considerable dietary limitations), and the importance of showing her a good time, became my primary concerns. I was a tireless companion. I fetched drinks, researched tours and co-ordinated the rotation of restaurants (there were three on the compound).

But mostly, I sat with my mother as she gazed at the water in the shade of a striped umbrella. All my childhood, I'd never once seen my mother lie in a lounge chair. I watched her bask in pleasure and relaxation, as rooted in the moment as any Buddhist devotee.

RICE & BEANS

"Deluxe restaurants are legion. One can dine comfortably but the price is high: never under six dollars." So wrote Jean-Paul Sartre in 1960, during his first visit to revolutionary Cuba.

These days, tourist food in Cuba is legendary for its badness. *No one goes to Cuba for the food,* is what everyone said to me, and yet, I had hope — that these amateur food critics had bypassed some of the simpler, more authentic fare. An obsession with food is the one thing my mother and I had in common.

Because it was easier for Vera, we ate most of our meals in the main buffet. My mother would sit herself down like a dowager on a transatlantic steamer voyage. With a certain hauteur, she'd send me off to get us some flute glasses of sparkling wine. Then we'd go foraging.

The buffet was huge, the variety impressive. Salad bar, soups, pasta bar, grills for meat and fish, and cafeteria-style offerings of pork, chicken, potatoes and rice. An enormous variety of desserts, and, to my mother's great delight, an ice cream sundae station (Cubans adore ice cream).

Sartre barely mentions food again in the account of his visit to the island, *Sartre on Cuba*. He describes a day spent with Fidel, in which the leader is given a lukewarm soft drink at a cabana on Varadero Beach. Fidel is indignant at this, not so much for his own discomfort, but because it reveals a lack of revolutionary consciousness. "If we don't do the maximum for the people at each beach," he says to the waitress, "the people will know we're not anxious enough to have them come, and they won't come. If someone doesn't do all he can all the time — and more — it's exactly as if he did nothing at all."

The problem with the food wasn't in the variety, and it certainly wasn't in the efforts of the workers on our behalf. It was in the taste. I had never known such a diverse array of foods to convey such dull sameness. Perhaps this is due to the *sofrito*, the main ingredient for almost every traditional Cuban dish; a sauté of onions, green peppers, garlic, oregano and bay leaves. Possibly it was also a mere illusion of variety. Most of the food offerings did not change from day to day, and this could have as much to do with the US embargo as with lack of imagination or will.

My mother and I always headed to the soup station first. Usually I had to locate a cook (I'd try a different one each time), hand him a bowl of, say, minestrone, and, in my bad Spanish, sweet-talk him into puréeing it. *Mi madre no puede comer solides.* (My mother can't eat solid food), I'd announce earnestly and with as much charm as I could muster. The cook, looking puzzled, offended or both, would disappear into the back with the bowl. After a very long time, perhaps half an hour, perhaps more, a waitress would find us. We never knew what to expect. Sometimes it was indeed the puréed version of the soup, with cream or some other ingredient added to make it tastier. At other times the soup would have vanished. There'd be a plate of mashed potatoes and gravy, or pureed squash, or something completely unrecognizable, in its place.

And then I'd begin my own hunt for food. After losing my attachment to novelty or flavour, I began to notice how fresh the food tasted. In fact, Cuba is a world leader in organic food production. This is born of necessity, since the

embargo prevents the import of most pesticides and her-
bicides. Natural bio-controls, like cut banana stems bait-
ed with honey to attract ants, are produced co-operatively.
These have proven to be more effective than chemicals.

Eating simply was the key. Crisp white rolls at breakfast,
with butter, cheese and apricot jam. The exquisite coffee. At
lunch you could compose a salad with fresh lettuces, green
beans, fish, capers, potatoes. The vegetables did not have the
metallic taste of North American salad bars. A successful dinner meant sticking to chicken or pork, pouncing on the fried
plantain when it was available and, of course, repeated trips to
the ice cream sundae station.

Sartre's visit to Cuba was said to have introduced a new
humanism into his philosophical practice. Che had read all of
Sartre's books: some say that, as a result, the Cuban revolution
was existentialist in its very conception. Sartre, for his part,
was enamoured of the practicality of a revolution that gave
its people not just freedom from colonialism but also literacy,
land, and medical care. Soon enough, however, both Sartre
and his wife, feminist philosopher Simone de Beauvoir, became critical of the repressive aspects of the Cuban regime.

But I wanted to hold on to my idealistic vision of Cuba.
Like my experience with food, I wanted to understand the
successes in balance with the disappointments. Like Sartre in
a 1960s France at war with Algeria, I too was disheartened
by my country's involvement in a foreign war. I wanted to be
won over too, if only for a time.

A few days into our trip, we took a bus tour into Havana.
It was an uncomfortable and fascinating experience, peering
at everyday Habanero life from the windows of a lumbering
tour bus. The Grand Theatre. The Malecón seawall, elegized

by Buena Vista Social Club. Old Havana, and its crumbling pastel beauty.

For lunch we were taken to an outdoor restaurant in the suburbs, a holding pen for Canadian tourists disgorged from tour buses. Still, it was a beautiful setting, with wooden tables set amid palm trees and gardens, a welcome relief from the heat of Havana's streets.

We sat at the long tables with couples from Regina, Surrey and Medicine Hat, all dressed, coincidentally, in Tilley wear. I listened to the plodding, predictable exchange: trips to the Bahamas, where the food had been much better; next year's plan to go to Mexico, more bang for your buck and no darn tax to pay at the airport. My mother smiled politely, too ladylike to complain in public. When the food arrived, we all fell upon it as though we had not eaten for days.

Nothing unusual: roasted pork with rice and beans. But the pork was so tender it was almost silken. It came with a mild but flavourful *jus* that made it melt in my mouth. The rice had been freshly prepared (as opposed to that which had been languishing in a buffet). The waitress took a shine to my ma, brought her puréed soup *and* mashed potatoes with gravy. My mother was the only one to get ice cream.

The rest of the day was a blur of colonial architecture, revolutionary monuments and the watercolour wash of this gorgeous, decaying city. I peered into a courtyard and saw a peacock walking gingerly down a set of stairs. I walked down a narrow street lined with iron balustrades, and chanced upon an outdoor concert of classical music. There were men selling used books, women selling melons and limes. I saw the word Fidel written in cursive script across a lemon-coloured wall.

The trip back was long and regretful. I wanted to stay, blend into the magic and sizzle of Havana. I had been won over.

I, CAMERA

Not long after arriving in Cuba, I realized I had forgotten to pack my camera.

Hmphh, said my mother. *Polysporin. But. No. Camera. Bug. Spray. But. No. Camera.*

How would this trip get remembered? These fragile, final few years with my mother, after all those years of being estranged. There were spaces large as continents between us. There was no way I could understand what it meant to have your body invaded by cancer. What it's like to eat only puréed foods, to wheeze constantly, to speak through a tube in your throat.

I knew that my mother would never fully understand the queer details of my life. The never quite fitting in, versus the detailed pleasures that outweighed all of that. What it's like to constantly edit those details in the classroom, in the lunchroom and in her very own kitchen. Rarely bringing my partners home for Christmas or Easter, because it just didn't seem worth the trouble it would cause.

My memory became the shutter of a lens, blinking constantly.

Whether because of the buttery light, the smoothness of the piña coladas or the abundance of ice cream, my mother was loquacious on this trip.

Time was slipping away. There were things she needed to tell me. Things I needed to ask.

Sometimes it was a lot of information to take in. Like the camera's aperture, I could feel myself opening up or closing down, depending on how painful the story. My mother talked about her marriage. For the first time, it seemed, she spoke frankly.

During that trip, I noticed how preoccupied people were with their cameras, sometimes, several to a table, conversations punctuated by the white hot flare of the flash. How, when we were in a tour bus entering Havana, the men across the aisle from us poised their cameras and phones aloft in a grasping, hungry gesture.

From time to time, I pulled out my sketchbook and my watercolours. I tried to paint a portrait of my mother sitting amid coconut palms, drinking her piña colada and reading the food memoir *Tastes Like Cuba*, which she regularly snatched from me. It was impossible to capture the contentment in my mother's face, her loose, relaxed posture as she reclined in a wicker chair.

I bought a disposable camera in a shop in Varadero, and a few grainy shots in the blue-red shades of 1960s Kodachrome, with a flare where the light leaked in, are what I managed to bring back.

The week after I returned, I told my students the story of forgetting my camera. I wanted to illustrate what Guy Debord has called "the society of the spectacle," the way we communicate, these days, through consumerism, via images and screens. One student told us about her dad, who went backpacking in the 1970s; for some reason, there are no photos of that time.

So he tells me the stories and I remember them, she said.

In Cuba, over our 5 p.m. cocktails (Mojito for me, Cuba Libre for her), my mother and I are dressed in our evening dining clothes. There is no rule about evening wear here, but I have taken a cue from my mother, who dons a beautifully coordinated outfit each evening.

Sipping her cocktail thoughtfully, my mother describes some scenes from her marriage. Mere description, no exposition. She could easily be talking about someone else's life.

I'd cook all Sunday morning, she said, *and then we went to church. On the way home we'd stop so he could get his Sunday* New York Times. *I'd serve a nice Sunday dinner. Then he'd go to the living room with his newspaper and he'd sit there all afternoon.* Her voice at this point contains withering scorn: *All. Afternoon. Reading. The. Newspaper.*

My mother's face is impassive after she tells me this, her lips flat-lined. I rise to get us more drinks.

When I return, she takes the drink and swallows it in one gulp. I am quiet for a moment, watching the serrated shadow of a palm tree against a pastel blue wall. All those years of Mama's chilling silence that I thought were my fault.

Did you ever think of leaving him? I ask.

She says nothing, and looks away.

My mother and I made the best of our disposable camera during the trip.

Me in shorts and a cowboy hat at the Plaza de la Revolución. My mother eating a chocolate ice cream sundae at the resort, a childlike grin on her face.

1950s cars, the streets of Old Havana. Graffiti: *Viva Fidel.*

My mother in an orange dress, lying on a chaise lounge on the white sand beach.

Arms outstretched, as though flying.

5.

ROUND DANCE

O Lord, grant rest to the soul of your departed servant, in a place of light, a place of green pasture, a place of refreshment, where all pain, sorrow, and sighing have fled away.
— Byzantine Litany of the Deceased

My cellphone vibrated in my pocket.

The timing was not good. I was in an Idle No More round dance in the middle of Dundas Square in Toronto. There was an older Indigenous woman to one side of me, a young Asian female university student to the other, and we were dancing, holding hands, in this blaring, advertisement-clogged concrete space. Idle No More, a grassroots protest movement begun by a group of Indigenous women, had spread across the country. Round dances — in shopping malls, government buildings and city squares — were its signature action. This dance was led by women. They held handmade placards. *Justice. Our Home and Native Land. We Are the Future and We Are Idle No More.*

I pulled out my phone, saw Taras's name on my cell, calling from Edmonton. I left the circle. I picked up. I figured he was calling about the live-in caregiver my mom had finally agreed to hire. I said, happily, *I'm in a round dance.*

Taras replied, in a voice as hollow and warped as a megaphone, *You need to sit down. Is there somewhere you can sit down?*

As soon as my brother said that, I knew.

The knowledge crept across the surface of my skin, entered my blood, and rearranged the very molecules of my body. I was thrust into some strange new body.

A body that had no mother.

The funny thing, and I found it funny even as it happened, was that everything should have stopped. The round dance continued; maybe it shouldn't have. Huge LED screens kept flashing lingerie ads, unbelievable. People slouched in metal chairs, drinking Tim Hortons coffee: how could they?

I walked, I walked, I walked across the square, dodging shoppers, homeless men and office workers, holding the cellphone to my ear. Why walk, I should have laid down. Noises came out of my throat, an *oh*, and a *no*, and then an *ohhhhhh-hhhhhhh*. What was the point of those noises, who had composed them? I didn't know. There was no future, and no past. I was walking. That was all.

The concrete was grey. The sky was grey. My brother's voice was as cold and grey as the concrete, but then it softened. *You need to sit down*, he kept saying.

You. Need. To. Sit. Down. Maybe he saw that on a medical show; that's what people say on medical shows. Why did an empty chair appear and why did I sit in it? My brother was still talking. Why was he still talking? But it was worse when the conversation ended and we said goodbye. I sat in the metal chair. My body folded over itself. I had to go home now, but I couldn't figure out how I would do this.

A man came by and asked, *You OK?* and kept walking. Why did he keep walking? A colleague of mine was in the round dance, filming it. She had looked so happy. I should have gone to tell her what happened. But it would make her sad, and anyways, I didn't know how I'd get there.

From far away I could hear the women drumming. An old, wounded heartbeat.

There would be a time when I would know how to leave the metal chair. It was getting colder. The winter light had a bruised, blue tinge. But I didn't want to leave the chair, not yet. Because everything should have stopped.

So I knew it was best, for now, to stay the fuck in that chair.

GREEN REMAINS

Taras met me at the airport in Edmonton. His awkward embrace lasted a second longer than usual, and I'm pretty sure I heard him say, *Good to see you.*

We picked up his son Stephan, and had a solemn Vietnamese pho lunch in a fluorescent-lit cavern. Stephan's round face was emoticon-sad. During lunch, he kept his eyes downcast, swallowing big gulps of soup. Taras and I chatted about Mom's caregiver candidates as though she were still alive. Taking care of my mother had bonded us over the years.

That last candidate you sent me seemed pretty good.

Yeah, I found her online. Lots of experience.

Don't know how Mom would deal with someone coming in for the whole day, though.

Who were we, if not a daughter and a son?

It was just three days since my mother had died at a Seniors' Adult Day Centre. She had collapsed in her chair, in the middle of Conversation Club. The resident doctor had tried to revive her, to no avail.

Must've have been a killer of a conversation. I said to my brother and nephew. No one laughed.

We paid the bill and drove to Mama's condo. None of us had been there since she'd died.

The three of us stood in the vestibule. Ma's blue slippers by the door, the ones Taras got her for Christmas. Overflowing basket of laundry in the hall. I could see her favourite nightgown, with its sprigs of flowers, on the top of the pile.

We were straining our ears for the sound of Ma shuffling on the carpet. Waiting for her to greet us and lead us to the kitchen.

I was aching for the smell of chicken stew.

The empty apartment came into focus. I'd never been anywhere as empty as that.

We walked around the large, light-filled rooms of Vera's condo. I picked up the cup of coffee she'd been drinking before she left for the centre. In the sink, a dirty bowl from the meal she'd had three nights before. Trousers on the bedroom floor, bed unmade, bright scarves thrown on the dresser, bathroom rock-star-messy as always.

Without a word, Taras and I set to work with garbage bags and started tossing things: pants, pajamas, the mounds of medical supplies it took to keep her swallowing and breathing.

I spent the night there.

In the morning, I stumbled into the kitchen, opened the fridge. The only things there were Ma's frozen meals on wheels. Broccoli casserole. Shepherd's pie. In the freezer: Tupperware containers of soups Taras had made, labelled with masking tape in his uneven hand. *Lentle Soup. Creme of Mushroom*. Misspelled and lovingly arrayed, covered in hoar frost.

I went in search of coffee. Careened across the black ice of a parking lot at 7 a.m.

Starbucks: closed. Returned to the condo. Sat on the couch, coat still on. Very soon, Mama would appear, with the brilliant, toothless smile she always bestowed when she woke up and found me, her prodigal daughter, in her living room.

I sat on the couch. I waited, patiently. Light came through the windows and moved across the room.

I went into her bedroom. There was her king-size bed, the floral quilt still tossed back, showing the scant rectangle of bed she slept in. There was a faint smell of perfume. There were only two things on the wall, a Byzantine icon of the Virgin Mary, and my mother's Bachelor of Arts Diploma, Carleton University, 1974.

I panned around the room, like a camera. Ironing board, a dishevelled pile of primary-coloured blouses still on it; wooden dresser covered in old photos and dusty jewelry boxes made of inlaid wood, from Ukraine; a shaky card table in the corner, covered with file folders. I walked toward it.

I pulled out one folder, sat on the unmade bed, opened the folder: yellow foolscap and old xeroxed documents, falling out like a drift of dirty snow. My grandmother's will, and the legal challenge my mother and my uncle had drummed up. Baba had left everything to Lily, her youngest daughter. My mother and Lily did not speak after that terrible injustice, that painful neglect: a parent favouring one child over the other.

Gruesomely fascinated, I went through papers as dry as parchment. Found a long letter, written in my mother's handsome penmanship, to Lily, just after her laryngectomy surgery. An attempt at reconciliation.

My husband has died. My son has died. I cannot speak. I cannot speak.

My mother had always protected us, her children, from her own feelings about her body's rude transformation. I never once heard her bemoan her fate. I read the entire letter, three pages long, plump with description.

I called my friend Janice.

I'll come pick you up right now, she said.

The next day, Taras, Jeannie and I met at the funeral director's office.

Jim, the funeral director, sat behind a polished desk. I was obscurely grateful that he'd dressed up for us in his grey double-breasted suit, blue and white striped tie and heavy silver watch. He was a portly, self-satisfied man, with a wry sense of humour and a smile that looked like a sneer. *Now that'll cost extra*, he'd deadpan, when we asked for tissues or water.

Jim was the kind of guy that met your serious with funny and your funny with serious. As we strolled through the showroom looking at coffins, I nervously, jokingly, asked if they offered organic funerals. Jim gave me a sober rundown of the latest green practices in the industry, including liquification, the current gold standard. After choosing flowers and a casket, Taras and I drove to the graveyard to make arrangements for the burial, discussing liquification along the way.

I wonder what they use to do it.

Probably, like, a huge juicer.

Do it yourself, save a ton of money.

We went back to Taras's place, a low-slung 1970s split-level. I offered to make dinner, Asian noodles. Taras pulled kilos of vegetables out of the fridge, way too much. I chopped them all: peppers, carrots, broccoli, mushrooms, bok choy, zucchini, gai lan. I made a peanut sauce and added several packages of rice noodles.

That's a lot of noodles, said Taras.

Lydia arrived from the airport with my niece Sonya. Stephan sleepily emerged from his bedroom. Jeannie arrived. There were stiff hugs and bare, single words. Everyone sat down at the table, fidgeting, or tapping at cellphones, or staring into space. I put the giant wok in the centre of the dining room table. Taras set out bowls and forks and torn pieces of paper towel.

Taras: *Anybody want beer?*

Jeannie: *Wine please.*

Michael: *Hey, this isn't bad.*

Lydia: *Wine.*

Sonya: *Definitely wine.*

Me: *I just threw it together.*

Michael: *Any vodka?*

Me: *There's more. I made too much.*

Taras: *Why don't I just liquefy it?*

Me: *Eew.*

We managed a family meal without Mama at the centre. We gulped those noodles down.

BREATHING NORMALLY

On January 11, 2013, Vera Anne Bociurkiw of Edmonton passed away at the age of 86 years. Vera was born in Schvaikivtsi, Ukraine, in 1927. She emigrated with her mother, Evhenia Wasylyshyn, and her brother Steve to Morinville, Alberta, in 1932 to join her father, Mikhailo Wasylyshyn. She married Bohdan Bociurkiw in Edmonton in 1950. Besides being a mother to six children, Vera Bociurkiw was also a student of French literature, an immigrant settlement worker, a gourmet cook and a world traveller. Her hospitality was renowned to all. Vera is survived by her loving children, Taras (Olya), Jeannie Lloyd, Marusya, Michael and Lydia; five grandchildren, Sonya, Natalie, Zorya (Patrick), Krystyna and Stephan; three great-grandchildren, Reece, Peyton and Owen; one brother and sister, Steve (Charlotte) and Lillian. Predeceased by husband Bohdan, son Roman and parents Michael and Eugenia.

—Vera Anne Bociurkiw: Obituary
The Ottawa Citizen, January 14, 2013

I was on the plane, on my way home from Edmonton. The safety video was playing. "Adjust your mask. Breathe normally." The voice-over lady sounded exhausted, as though she had been trying to breathe normally for a very long time.

I was bringing a box of my mother's stuff with me. Mama's china set. My inheritance.

At airport security, I'd loaded the box of my mother's Royal Doulton china and crystal onto a conveyor belt. I turned and looked at the screen that showed the box's x-ray. Pink, yellow, blue and green pastels, like Easter.

My mother died, I said, by way of unnecessary explanation, to the guard. *This is her china set.*

I'm very sorry, said the guard, in a thick East European accent. The guard and I stared solemnly at the x-ray screen.

Did you put paper between the bowls? she asked.

I assured her that I had.

But in the x-ray image, stemware floated merrily in space, askew. Bowls huddled together. A vase stood alone.

An x-ray of dinner parties, faculty receptions, family events. I could hear an audio track of glasses tinkling, and satisfied male laughter.

I could see the vase that held the flowers I sent on Mother's Day. The liqueur glasses that my father filled with Cointreau at Christmas. The platter that held the Christmas turkey, the plates that had served the cabbage rolls and the perogies, the gravy urn from which Mama ladled her delicious mushroom sauce. Tables set, dishes washed, again and again and again. A history of celebrations. An archive of duty and loss, piling up over the years. My grandmother's enchanting stories and simple recipes; my father's erudite language and scholarship; my brother's unbearably sad music that floated in the air of Vancouver like dustmotes; my mother's cooking: all vanished.

I wondered if my mother had enjoyed any of it.

But she had asked me, twice, before she died, to take care of her china. There it all was, fragile, and in its constituent pieces, lots of paper between the bowls, on the x-ray machine screen.

It's the only thing of value that I have, she'd said.

BLESSING

O purify me, then I shall be clean; O wash me, I shall be whiter than snow.
— Psalm 51:7

The weeks following my mother's death bloom with spectacular regret, my body tangling in sheets and quilt, pillows and legs every which way.

On one such *nuit blanche*, I go downstairs, sit on the couch and listen to the trains' high-pitched screams as they move along the tracks across the street. The digital clock in the kitchen shoves the minutes forward: 3:11 a.m. Plenty of time on my hands, so I trace the contours of all my failures, large and small. Various professorial gaffes return to haunt me. Like the time I showed up two hours late for Women and Film because my Ikea clock had stopped (this was before cellphones; that clock was the only timekeeper I owned). The students were running the class quite efficiently without me. One was lecturing, another was scribbling things on the blackboard. They regarded me with sadness as I took my place at the lectern.

Clearly, they did not believe my story.

Once I've gone over all the old, familiar embarrassments and regrets, I really get into it. I roll up my sleeves for a palooza of remorse. The loss of my mother, and the scant decade of closeness we had. The times I was impatient, or controlling. The fact that we never got to say goodbye.

I had been counting on a farewell, a good one. There hadn't been one with my grandmother. *Te ne ye rodyna.* You are not my family, the last words my baba, whom I'd loved all my life, said to me.

Blessed are they who show mercy; mercy shall be theirs.
— Beatitudes

Years ago, I took my mother to St. Mary's Ukrainian Catholic Church in Vancouver for Sunday mass. During his sermon, the priest started ranting angrily about Catholicism's trifecta of evil: abortion, euthanasia and homosexuality. I looked over at Mama. Her face was sleepy, peaceful. I walked out in protest. Strode around the block, got a takeout coffee at Starbuck's and realized I had to go back to get my mother.

Asked her, afterwards. What she thought. *God. Loves. Homosexuals. And. Heterosexuals*, she proclaimed. Like she'd just been on the phone with Jesus.

I didn't believe her. Why would I?

Mama went so quickly, no care home, no palliative ward, no long cinematic goodbye, me at her bedside saying wise things to her, or her to me. She skipped the final chapters. She always was impetuous that way. It felt like the worst snub. Hadn't I worked so hard for us to be on good terms when she died?

What were Mama's last words to me?

I had come for a week that time, found colleagues to teach my classes for me. She wasn't deathly ill, but she was frail. Something told me to go.

September in Edmonton. Elm trees lining every street, the city illuminated with gold. I was cruise director; we went out every day. To the farmers' market, to the art gallery.

To her favourite consignment store (she bought a sharp leather jacket). I set up a literary reading, thought my mom would enjoy that. She made chocolate marble Bundt cake. Brought it to the bookstore. Graciously passed it around afterwards, to the pleasure and bemusement of all.

To the shopping mall, to the movies, even a road trip to Vegreville with its hilariously giant Easter egg, pale green prairie fields all the way there, my niece Natalie at the wheel, baby Owen snoozing in the back, Mama silent, riding shotgun, glad to be on the road.

We did so much she got exhausted. Became pale, shaky, scared. I had to call the doctor. A weekend of rest, in an elder facility, not quite a hospital. I went to see her there just before I caught my plane. She had dressed for me, chartreuse jacket and black trousers, silk floral scarf as usual at her throat. I faux-apologized for wearing her out. She gave me a wry look. I started to say goodbye.

She took my hands. *I. Love. You. And. I. Respect. You.* She said it twice, *I. Love. You. And. I. Respect. You.*

Why did she say it twice? Why respect? Why not just love?

In that moment, in that white, narrow hospital room, I did not believe her.

The clock flips to 5 a.m. I head upstairs. Lying in bed, I hear the faraway swoosh of streetcars coming to life. Like the yellow sweep of car lights illuminating a darkened room, I am struck with sudden revelation.

Her final words. Her blessing.

CODA: FIVE YEARS LATER

I can still hear my mother's beautiful, ravaged voice in my head: that deep no-bullshit chord of survival. I recognize her wry smile in the mirror, and I feel my body taking on the maternal heft of her gestures: the way I spoon food onto the plates of those who dine at my table; the way I cross my arms, sit back, and listen to a friend's high-risk academic tales.

I can sometimes recall the toasty smell of browned butter sizzling luxuriously around bread crumbs, which coated the green beans Mama made for Sunday lunch. My mother owned a copy of Julia Child's *Mastering the Art of French Cooking* — is that why she cooked with so much butter? Her hands, astonishingly slender and graceful, ladled stew over perogies and placed them in front of me like a hat trick, as if the labour to make them was insignificant. Love, never verbally expressed, was in every component of that gesture.

Who will ever cook for me like that again?

My kitchen is pungent with onion, garlic and olive oil sautéeing in a pan, the base for minestrone soup, for mushroom pasta, for chickpea curry. My kitchen smells of root vegetables roasting in the oven, slathered with rosemary, lemon and sea salt, a winter go-to when I'm blank with fatigue. There is the honeyed aroma of fruit pie, the only thing I ever bake; of the musky scent of granola I mix up every few months. Recently, I shared my house and my kitchen with two young lesbian refugees. My kitchen smelled constantly of meat fried in olive oil, the only thing these women considered to be a meal.

They had lost so much, these girls, yet they laughed and cooked incessantly, their cooking part lament, part delirium. Like my mother and my grandmother, they understand food to be the only country that is truly theirs.

Mourning happens in stages; it is a work-in-progress. My mother has become part of the celestial system. I hope it does not cause the reader concern if I confess that my mother speaks to me, in dreams and in prayers, and sometimes on the streetcar, too. She tells me to have compassion, or to let someone go, or: *You. Should. Have. A. Party*.

During the final years of her life, I read to my mother from my own work, in hospital rooms, in living rooms, and in waiting rooms. Mama's face like bleached wrinkled cotton, lifted toward the sound of my sentences. *You write so beautifully,* she said.

I have found that the only way to survive loss is to integrate it into every part of your life. To, in a sense, refuse loss. To maintain a place for the dead among the living, as Ukrainians with their graveyard visits, their place settings for the dead, and their gossip of death, do. To breathe it in, as the Buddhists would say. And thus, to avoid melancholia. Perhaps, even, to find gratitude.

One dull March of chill winds and tree branches scratched across a mottled sky, I head to the country to visit Marc. There is a crackling fire and a pewter grey lake is visible through the kitchen window. There is a dog named Leroy who puts his handsome head on my lap. There is space and time. I haven't been eating and I haven't been cooking. I've given my body and soul to my job. It is Easter, but without my mother it is a meaningless holiday, best left unmarked.

Marc places food in front of me with her brusque and tender hands. Roast lamb. Homemade bread. Hot cross buns.

The food is voluble, expressive in every way. It says: love
—steady, serviceable, healthy love — is ordinary and quite
splendid.

It says: your mother is with you and always will be.

RECIPES

FUDGE RIBBON PIE

Adapted from *Better Homes and Gardens New Cook Book*

2-ounce squares unsweetened chocolate
6-ounce can evaporated milk (⅔ cup)
1 cup sugar
1 Tbsp. butter or margarine
1 tsp. vanilla
1 quart peppermint ice cream
9-inch baked pastry shell, cooled
3 egg whites
½ tsp. vanilla
¼ tsp. cream of tartar
6 Tbsp. sugar
3¼ Tbsp. crushed peppermint stick candy

In saucepan, combine chocolate and evaporated milk. Cook and stir over low heat until chocolate is melted, about 15 minutes. Stir in the 1 cup sugar and butter. Cook over medium heat until thickened, 5 to 8 minutes longer, stirring occasionally. Stir in 1 teaspoon vanilla. Cool.

Spoon half of the ice cream into the cooled pastry shell. Cover with half the cooled chocolate sauce; freeze. Repeat with remaining ice cream and sauce. Cover and freeze overnight or until firm.

Prepare meringue by beating egg whites with ½ teaspoon vanilla and cream of tartar until soft peaks form. Gradually add 6 tablespoons of sugar, beating until stiff and glossy peaks form.

Fold 3 Tbsp. crushed candy into meringue. Spread meringue over chocolate layer and seal to edge. Sprinkle with remaining candy. Freeze for several hours or until firm.

Bake at 475 degrees for 3 to 4 minutes or until meringue is lightly browned. Cover loosely and return to freezer for several hours before serving. Serves 8.

STUFFED BAKED EGGPLANT

From *The Vegetarian Epicure*

3 medium-size eggplants
2 red bell peppers
3 to 5 Tbsp. olive oil
Salt and pepper
1 clove garlic, minced
2 onions
3 to 4 sprigs fresh parsley and basil
3 to 4 tomatoes

Topping:
1 cup ground walnuts
½ cup wheat germ
¾ cup grated Parmesan cheese
2 Tbsp. melted butter
1 cup milk or light cream

Slice each eggplant in half lengthwise and cut out the meat, leaving a ¼-inch-thick shell. Dice the scooped-out eggplant into fairly large pieces, and the red pepper into small pieces, reserving about ⅓ of the peppers for decoration.

In a large skillet, sauté the eggplant and red pepper in about 3 tablespoons of the olive oil until evenly coated and slightly softened. Season with salt, pepper and garlic. Divide this mixture evenly among the 6 eggplant shells.

Chop the onion, parsley and tomatoes. Sauté the onions in the remaining olive oil, adding parsley, chopped basil and garlic. When onions get soft, add chopped tomatoes, simmer a few moments and spread on top of eggplant mixture in shells, patting it down. Shells should be full to the top but not overflowing.

Finally, combine wheat germ, ground nuts and Parmesan; moisten with melted butter and enough milk to make a soft paste, and spread a thin layer on top of each eggplant half. Decorate this crust with the reserved red pepper, sliced into thick strips.

Bake eggplants in an oiled dish for about 45 minutes at 350 degrees. Serve very hot.

WHOLE WHEAT POPPYSEED BREAD

Adapted from *Recipes for a Small Planet*

4½ cups lukewarm water
2 Tbsp. baking yeast
½ cup oil (canola is good)
½ cup honey
1 Tbsp. salt
1 Tbsp. crushed poppy seeds
2½ cups white unbleached flour
8–10 cups whole wheat flour

Put the lukewarm water in a large mixing bowl that will hold all of the bread when it is mixed. Sprinkle the yeast over the liquid and let it sit for about 5 minutes until it dissolves or puffs (different strains do different things). Then stir the mixture.

Add the oil, honey, salt and poppy seeds, stirring until the salt and honey have disappeared.

In a separate bowl, blend the flours thoroughly. Add the flour to the liquid 1–2 cups at a time. After about 4 cups are added, stir the batter about 100 times to develop the gluten in the wheat. Then, keep adding flour until the dough is kneadable (i.e., can be handled easily and doesn't stick to your hands.)

Cover the dough with a cloth and let the dough rest for about 15 minutes.

On a floured wooden board or countertop, flatten the dough with your hands, pushing it away from you; fold it in half, turn a ¼ turn, flatten again, fold and turn. Keep doing this until bread is smooth and elastic, about 10 minutes.

Place bread back in mixing bowl, cover, put it in a warm place and let rise until doubled, about 1 hour.

Preheat oven to 350 degrees.

Punch the dough down in the bowl, turn onto floured surface, and knead a couple of minutes until easy to handle, adding flour if too sticky. Divide the dough into 4 pieces and dust about 1 tablespoon of flour over them. Drop dough into the bottom of 4 oiled coffee cans (or 46-ounce juice cans). Let rise one more time (slightly less than double their size).

Place cans in preheated oven. After baking for 35 minutes, remove one loaf from the oven. Tap the top; if it sounds hollow, it's done. If it doesn't, put it back in for another few minutes.

Makes 4 loaves.

VEGGIE TOFU STIR-FRY WITH ORANGE GINGER GLAZE

Adapted from Mollie Katzen's website

This is an updated, fancier form of stir-fry that you could, perhaps, serve at at a retro dinner party.

The Glaze:
½ cup orange juice (from 1 medium orange)
2 Tbsp. cider vinegar
1 Tbsp. soy sauce
1 Tbsp. brown sugar or honey
1 Tbsp. minced fresh ginger
2 tsp. minced garlic (2 good-sized cloves)
1 tsp. toasted sesame oil
½ tsp. red pepper flakes
1 Tbsp. cornstarch

The Stir-fry:
1 pound firm tofu, cut into ¾-inch cubes
2 Tbsp. canola, soy or peanut oil
1 medium onion, cut into large (1½-inch) square slices
¾ tsp. salt
2 medium carrots, sliced on the diagonal (¼-inch thick)
½ a medium head cauliflower, in 1-inch florets (about 3 cups)
½ a medium head broccoli, chopped (about 3 cups)
About 15 mushrooms, stems trimmed, if necessary, wiped clean and quartered
2 small zucchini (one yellow, one green), chopped or diced
1 medium red bell pepper, cut into 1-inch squares

Combine all the glaze ingredients (except the cornstarch) in a liquid measuring cup with a spout, and whisk until blended. Place the cornstarch in a small bowl, and drizzle in about ¼ cup of the glaze, whisking constantly until the cornstarch is dissolved. (The mixture will be cloudy.) Pour this solution back into the measuring cup, whisking it in. Set aside, leaving the whisk in the cup.

Put a large pot of cold water to boil over high heat, and place a colander in the sink. When the water boils, add the tofu and reduce the heat to medium-low. Simmer the tofu for 10 minutes, then gently pour it into the colander and let it drain. Set aside.

Have all the vegetables and the simmered tofu cut and in bowls or containers near the stove. Place a wok or large, deep skillet over medium heat and wait about a minute. Pour in 1 tablespoon of the oil, and swirl to coat the pan (or just push the oil around with a wok spatula or serving spoon). Turn the heat to high, add the onion and ¼ teaspoon of the salt, and stir-fry for 1 minute. Add the other tablespoon of oil, plus the carrot, cauliflower and broccoli, and another ¼ teaspoon of the salt. Keep the heat high and the vegetables moving, and stir-fry for approximately 2 minutes, or until the broccoli turns bright green and shiny.

Add the mushrooms and tofu and the remaining ¼ teaspoon of salt. Keep the heat high, and continue to stir-fry for another minute, mixing all the vegetables up from the bottom of the pan. Add the zucchini and bell pepper, and cook one more minute.

Whisk the glaze to reincorporate the cornstarch (it will have settled to the bottom), then quickly pour the whole cupful into the wok or skillet. Cook and stir for just about a minute more. The glaze will coat everything and thicken a little. Serve immediately.

For authenticity, serve with brown rice.

JANE'S MUSHROOM SOUP

2 oz. dried mushrooms (e.g., porcini)
2 Tbsp. butter
1 cup finely chopped onion
1 lb. fresh mushrooms, sliced (about 5 cups, can be a mix of wild and cultivated)
¼ cup flour
salt and freshly ground pepper
2 cups broth (beef, chicken or veg)
1 cup heavy cream or sour cream (optional)
¼ cup sherry (optional)

Place the dried mushrooms in a bowl and add boiling water to cover. Let stand until thoroughly softened.

Melt butter in saucepan and add onions. Cook until wilted and add fresh mushrooms. Stir and cook until wilted.

Sprinkle with flour, salt and pepper to taste. Stir to coat the mushrooms, then add to broth.

Drain the dried mushrooms and measure the soaking liquid. Add enough water to make two cups. Add this and the dried mushrooms to saucepan. Simmer for about 15 minutes.

Purée the mushrooms, using a food processor or electric blender. Return to heat and bring to a boil. Add the cream if desired. Chill and serve cold, or serve piping hot.

Optional: add sherry or other wine just before serving.

Yields about 6 servings.

HEARTY LENTIL SOUP

This is not the Carnegie Centre's soup. It is a recipe adapted from *Cook's Illustrated* magazine. In this (semi-vegetarian) version, the lentils don't get mushy, because of the way in which they are "sweated" when they go into the acidic tomato base. This is the best lentil soup I've ever made. I think Roman would have liked it too.

1 large onion, chopped fine
2 medium carrots, chopped fine
3 medium garlic cloves, smashed & chopped
1 tsp. ground cumin
1 tsp. cinnamon
1 tsp. ground coriander
1 14-oz. can of diced tomatoes
1 bay leaf
2 Tbsp. minced fresh basil or thyme
1 cup lentils (black, brown or green), rinsed
1 tsp. salt, pepper to taste
½ cup dry white wine
4½ cups low-sodium chicken or vegetable broth
1½ cups water
1½ tsp. lemon juice
3 Tbsp. minced fresh parsley leaves

Sauté onion and carrots in large stockpot until soft. Add garlic and spices; cook, stirring contantly, until fragrant, about 1 minute. Add tomatoes and bay leaf; cook until simmering. Stir in lentils, salt and pepper to taste; cover and simmer for about 10 minutes. Uncover, increase heat to high, add wine and bring to simmer. Add chicken broth and water; bring to a boil, cover partially and reduce heat to low. Simmer until lentils are tender but still hold their shape, 30 to 40 minutes, depending on the type of lentil you are using. With a hand-held blender, purée some of the soup. Stir in lemon juice and parsley and heat until hot, about 5 minutes.

DARK CHOCOLATE ICE CREAM WITH SEA SALT

Adapted from the blog *Coffee & Quinoa*

2 cups whole milk
2 cups heavy cream
½ cup cocoa powder
¾ cup sugar
8 egg yolks
1½ tsp. sea salt
1 tsp. vanilla extract
2 Tbsp. brewed coffee

In a saucepan over medium heat, whisk together milk, cream, cocoa powder and sugar until cocoa powder is thoroughly incorporated and sugar is dissolved.

In a medium bowl, whisk together egg yolks. Slowly pour in about ½ cup of the chocolate mixture, whisking constantly, to temper. Pour in the rest of the chocolate mixture, then return to saucepan over medium heat.

Heat, stirring constantly with a wooden spoon, until the mixture reaches 175 degrees. At this point, you should be able to draw a line with your finger across the back of the spoon and have it stay.

Pour mixture through a strainer into a bowl. Stir in the sea salt, vanilla extract and coffee. Bring down to room temperature, then cover and refrigerate until thoroughly chilled, at least several hours and up to overnight.

Churn in an ice cream machine according to manufacturer's instructions. Scoop into a separate container, cover and freeze several hours more, until hardened. Makes 4-6 servings.

BABA'S CHICKEN STEW

This dish is, of course, traditionally eaten with perogies, but it would probably be delicious with egg noodles or mashed potatoes too.

4 chicken thighs, skin removed
1 Tbsp. vegetable oil or butter
2 Tbsp. flour
2 garlic cloves, finely chopped
1½ cups low-sodium chicken stock

In a medium saucepan, fry chicken thighs in oil until well browned, about 5-10 minutes. Add flour, mixing in well, until lightly browned. Add chicken stock and minced garlic, mixing well. Let this mixture come to a slow boil until thickened, stirring all the while. Cover and simmer for about 1 hour until chicken is soft. Serves 4.

CREAM OF BROCCOLI SOUP

1 head of broccoli, chopped
1 onion, chopped
2 potatoes, cubed
4 stalks of celery, chopped
2 cups of chicken or vegetable stock
1 cup soya milk (whole milk can be substituted)
½ tsp. reshly ground black pepper
pinch of nutmeg
1 head roasted garlic
1 tsp. dried thyme
2 tsp. olive oil

Heat olive oil in a pot on medium heat, add onion and celery, sauté until translucent. Add potatoes, broccoli, celery, salt, pepper, spices and chicken stock. Simmer on low heat until vegetables become soft.

Squeeze the roasted garlic into the mixture. Place soup in blender (or use immersion blender in pot) and purée. Add more stock if you like it to be less dense.

Makes about 6 servings.

CUBAN RICE & BEANS

Adapted from *Tastes Like Cuba* by Eduardo Machado, this dish is known to Cubans as Moros y Cristianos, which translates as Moors and Christians. According to Machado, the black beans represent the Moors (Black people) and the white rice the Christians. He writes: "Its name comes from the Spaniards who occupied Cuba in the 1500s. The reference dates to the Moorish occupation of the Iberian Peninsula between the eighth and fifteenth centuries. Occupations and conquests, racial and holy wars, all in one little dish…"

½ pound thick-cut bacon, sliced into 1-inch pieces (optional for vegetarians)
1 Spanish onion, peeled and chopped
½ green pepper, stems and seeds removed, chopped
¼ cup canned tomato sauce
1½ tsp. salt
½ tsp. ground black pepper
1 tsp. dried oregano
½ tsp. ground cumin
2 cups medium-grain rice
2 15.5-ounce cans black beans, drained and rinsed thoroughly (Machado suggests making your own black beans, but that's your call)
4 cups chicken or vegetable broth

Fry the bacon in a large pot or Dutch oven over medium-high heat until crispy, about 6 minutes. Transfer to a plate using a slotted spoon.

Add the onion and green pepper to the pot and cook, stirring until softened slightly, about 3 minutes. Add the garlic and cook, stirring, 1 minute more. Add the tomato sauce, salt, black pepper, oregano and cumin. Stir and cook 1 minute more.

Add the rice, beans and half the bacon to the pot, along with the broth. Bring to a boil. Reduce the heat to low and simmer, covered, until the rice is cooked through, the beans are soft and the flavours have blended, about 25 minutes. Fluff the rice with a fork, then stir gently to make sure the beans are evenly distributed. Serve garnished with the remaining bacon sprinkled over the top. Makes 8–10 servings.

PEANUT SAUCE

Adapted from the *Moosewood Cookbook*

1 cup chopped onion
2 cloves crushed garlic
1 cup good-quality peanut butter
1 Tbsp. honey
½ tsp. cayenne pepper
juice of 1 lime
1-2 tsp. freshly grated ginger
1 bay leaf
1 Tbsp. cider vinegar
3 cups water
½ - 1 tsp. salt
dash of soya sauce
1 Tbsp. sesame oil

In a saucepan, sauté the onions, garlic, bay leaf and ginger in the sesame oil, lightly salted. When the onion becomes translucent, add remaining ingredients. Mix thoroughly, Simmer on lowest possible heat 30 minutes, stirring occasionally.

Makes enough for 6–8 servings of noodles.

MARUSYA BOCIURKIW is a writer, filmmaker and professor. She is the director of ten films, and the author of six books and over fifty scholarly, popular and arts-based articles. Her recent film *This Is Gay Propaganda: LGBT Rights & the War in Ukraine* has screened in twelve countries and has been translated into three languages. Her books have won and been shortlisted for several awards, including the CBC Literary Award, a Lambda Literary Award and the Independent Publisher Award. She is Co-Director of the Studio for Media Activism & Critical Thought at Ryerson University in Toronto. She is one of the recipients of the 2018 Kobzar Literary Award, as well as receiving Ryerson's Knowledge Mobilization & Engagement Award in 2018. In her teaching, writing and filmmaking, she works at the intersection of art, social justice, collaboration and friendship.